W9-AAS-972

Winchester-Frederick County Historical Society

JOURNAL

2017

Volume XXVIII

Cover: William Beamer, WWII Veteran

ISBN # 13: 978-1717246554
    # 10: 17172466559

Printed in the United States of America

Contents

Winchester-Frederick County Historical Society
1340 S. Pleasant Valley Road
Winchester, Va 22601
540/662-6550
www/winchesterhistory.org

About this Issue

In this twenty-eighth volume of the *Winchester-Frederick County Historical Society Journal,* we continue the series of oral history interviews with World War II veterans. This interview is with William Beamer who attended Douglas High School and enlisted in the U.S. Army in 1944. He served in a construction company in the Philippines and later in Korea. Bill Austin, retired U.S. Air Force pilot and public affairs officer and volunteer at Cedar Creek and Belle Grove National Historical Park, has researched the life of Thomas Laws, a Clarke County slave who carried messages between General Philip Sheridan and Winchester resident Rebecca Wright.

Gene Schultz pursued the story of how the Winchester and Frederick County World War One memorial came to be. Marcus Lemasters, an amateur archeologist led a team on an archeological dig on the Abram's Delight grounds. His report revealed some interesting information about their findings

As always, these articles tell us the stories of our area's people and its institutions. The publication of these items ensures that this history will be preserved, and that these voices will continue to be heard.

William Beamer, WWII Veteran

Oral History Interviews of
World War II Veterans

William Beamer

*Interview conducted by Harold Phillips,
January 17, 2002*

Phillips: Where were you born?

Beamer: I was born right here in Winchester, right here on Clifford Street. There I lived till I was about twelve years old and then I ended up on Kent Street. There I went to Douglas High School and worked after school, places like Boyd's Drug Store, delivering packages and stuff like that.

Phillips: Did you get to finish school?

Beamer: No, it was eleven grades, I went to the tenth and after that I ended up signing up to go to the Army; that was in 1944. I took my training in Aberdeen, Maryland, with the ordinance ammunition outfit and field training I took in Camp Pickett, Virginia. At that time we would convoy from Aberdeen, Maryland, to Camp Pickett and do six weeks of field training. Came back to Aberdeen which I was given what they called delay—enroute to California. I spent fifteen days in Winchester and I had six days to get to Sacramento, California. Once I got to California I went to a base called Camp Beale in California, where we took hand-to-hand combat training. Stayed there for about two months and then we got on a ship and left there and went for twenty-eight days. We were traveling and about half way through they told us we were going to the Philippine Islands.

Phillips: What was the basic training like?

Beamer: In Aberdeen?

Phillips: No, when you went down south.

Beamer: At Camp Pickett?

Phillips: Yeah.

Beamer: That was just mostly compass training, picking out points, finding certain points. If you wanted to go places and be able to find that, and things to do about stars which I never did learn much about but that was mostly what that was, learning your way around like in a jungle-type atmosphere.

Phillips: Did you get your weapons training at Aberdeen?

Beamer: Yeah, I did at Aberdeen.

Phillips: What was the hand-to-hand combat training like?

Beamer: I liked it. I didn't mind the hand-to-hand. I got used to it. Being a small person I was handling a lot of big people and so I got along with that pretty good. After that we went back; I was part of a company of carpenters. We would build a bridge across a ravine and we had a certain time to build it and it had to be built so a tank could run over it and we had some problems with that a couple a times. But after a while we could. Now I don't remember the time but depending on the size of the ravine we got pretty good at building it. If they say tanks were coming in six hours, we could almost have it ready for them when they got there.

Phillips: Were there any incidents aboard ship on your way to the Philippines?

Beamer: The only incident I had, I stayed sick. It took twenty-eight days to get to the Philippines 'cause we were back and forth, back and forth and somebody would say submarine is over there and never knew really what was going on cause we were a bunch of sick troops on a Navy ship. But it took so long to get there and I could not get used to the water. I stayed sick for twenty-eight days.

Phillips: Did you have to stay below most of the time or could you go on deck?

Beamer: You got up on deck for exercise on certain times. Sometimes we exercised with the sailors and we could come up and they were firing back at targets and we would come up, watch them and then we would go back below deck.

Phillips: When did you get to the Philippines?

Beamer: We got to the Philippines in June of 1945.

Phillips: What unit were you assigned to?

Beamer: We were with a engineering group, which you got to realize then we mostly dealt with companies. Because then the engineering group we were assigned to all of it was segregated, so we weren't in their company but we would be two or three miles from where our battalion headquarters was, so we dealt mostly in companies. We would get to a place and they would say Company B 590 you will go to Angeles up near Clark field and most of our work was done in company-like atmosphere.

Phillips: So when you got to the Philippines what landing was already made after the invasion?

Beamer: We went in after the Marines went through and they told us that the theater was closed and that meant we couldn't get any battle stars or anything like that even though snipers were still around. Guys were getting killed. The theater was closed for combat as we called it but I stayed in the Philippines for twelve months.

Phillips: Is this where you had to do a lot of the bridge building?

Beamer: No, that was just training in Aberdeen we did to build bridges. When I got to the Philippines we were put into a company; we had nothing but 105mm shells and we were running three shifts taking those shells off the ships and we'd put them in a dump and had them there. The dump to me seemed like it was big as Winchester. I never seen so many shells, but once we got that done, got all the shells in, we were just in a company I was what you called company carpenter. My job was to build cause we had no place to stay but tents. Then I started building. We used the tent and lumber around and wooden floors and I had 35 Philippine carpenters which were paid for by the Army. I had 50 Japanese prisoners; we used to clear areas where we were going to build the buildings. We would requisition prisoners like you would a Semi and go over and pick them up.

Phillips: Did they provide guards for the prisoners too?

Beamer: They had their own guards, like in the area where we were building. We had some problems with guards who were violent toward the prisoners but we handled that pretty good. I made it clear to the guards who were working for me at the time that I would bring anybody up for court martial that I caught doing something violent to the prisoners. That's the way it was told to me when you take them out you were supposed to see that they were treated all right and they were fed and brought back to the prison camp at night, so we got along pretty good with that. I had a nice company and a nice officer, company commander. Then things changed when they dropped the first atomic bomb.

Phillips: Were your officers white or black?

Beamer: White, all white officers.

Phillips: Then they dropped the atomic bomb.

Beamer: They dropped the first bomb and then the second bomb and then Japan surrendered. We were there thinking we were going to get to come home. And then it came down you had to have so many points and at that time I didn't have any children or battle stars so that meant I didn't have a whole lot of points. So the next thing I knew after being there for 12 months, in February I landed in South Korea in khaki clothes with snow about two feet deep and no place to really stay. We had a little small pup tent and then we found some old burned out bicycle shops which had a lot of bicycle buildings and we used those for living quarters until I got around to building more places to live. So I built in the Philippines, then I ended up building in Korea; but I only stayed for about five months. Then at that time it was my time to come home, we got to Seattle, Washington, must have been in July or August of 1946.

Phillips: Was there a lot of devastation in Korea?

Beamer: Oh yea, a lot of burned-out buildings, some of the buildings that we lived in had no roof but we could cover them with canvas on the sides if we found one with a pretty good roof and then we'd take 55 gallon drums of oil and run 'em in the buildings and we had little stoves and that's where the heat was. You didn't get a lot of heat but you didn't freeze; did that until I got enough buildings built while I was there that everybody was using the larger one—like eight men to a tent or building, but you had wooden floors and they had heat. But that's when I left and it took me 11 days to get from Korea to Seattle.

Phillips: Was your unit in Korea still off-loading ammunition?

Beamer: No.

Phillips: What did they do there?

Beamer: In Korea we didn't do too much of anything. Once we got there it was a matter of guarding depot where we had a lot of equipment. Back in them days they didn't let us be MPs but we guarded the depots because the Koreans could carry away a whole depot in a night's time. I never seen people carry so much stuff. So instead of putting MP on our helmets they put DP on there "Depot Police," and that's the way it ran most of the time; it was a lot of segregation back in that time. We had to put up with it, some officers. I guess it's like it is anywhere, like maybe Winchester would be, you had good people, people who would treat you right and do the best they could with the laws there at that time and I was lucky enough to get some good ones.

Phillips: Were there any accidents while you were off-loading down in the Philippines?

Beamer: Not really accidents, we ended up, one of fellows had to shoot a Filipino because some of the shells were wrapped in this white parachute stuff. The shells were wrapped in them and they used them to make clothing and they would come in at night and take these boxes which were about the size of those shells and bust them open and take all the cloth out of them. Well one of the guards shot one of the Filipinos. The job we had was to protect those things, shot a Filipino for taking one and was almost court-martialed for it but you didn't know.

But after that we went back to the company and Lieutenant Barnett, which was a nice officer, he went to battalion headquarters and wanted to know why I was being transferred and they came up with something had to do occupational duty after everything was over and in Korea I played on the baseball team and we just mostly traveled like from Inchon to Ansong City and Kempo Airfield. We would have to deliver stuff up there to Kempo that was almost 60 to 70 miles and we would take them up and that wasn't too bad unless you got behind a bunch of those honey-drippers and that in the summer time and about 20 or 30 of them in front of you and you couldn't pass that was awful.

Phillips: Did you ever get up to Weehonbu?

Beamer: No, I was in Seoul, places like that, we weren't allowed near the Thirty-eighth Parallel.

Phillips: Is it right on the Thirty-eighth Parallel?

Beamer: Yeah. We weren't allowed to go there because after we got there we didn't have—well the war was over, but we didn't have any weapons. The only thing we had was the "billy clubs" and that's what we guarded at depots with were "billy clubs." I got back to Seattle and Fort Lewis and from there we traveled by troop train to Fort Bragg, North Carolina, and that is where I ran into more segregation. We were checking in all of our stuff and they were checking in all of the white troops first. After all of them went through, they checked us and told us before we got on the bus to police the area. So there were some fellows in there that said no, we are not going to police the area; all these people been here and dropped all these cigarette butts and things and we are not going to pick them up. Well, they wouldn't bus us back to where we where supposed to go, so we all got together and walked, walked back and it came out at Fayetteville and I got my discharge signed by President Truman. "Through these portals passed the best soldiers in the world." I got out to the train getting ready to get on the train and the man says your car is full; you can't get on the train. I said what am I suppose to do? Well I was with some white soldiers I played baseball with in Korea. We had a team. They told the conductor he is with us, he is going on the train. I was in the middle so I didn't know what to do and they had state troopers down there because evidently that had happened before. So the state trooper came over to me because at that time I was the only black one right there getting a diss that was coming and he took me to the side and told me now don't get yourself in trouble. Don't let these men get you in trouble; he said there are laws down here and they are probably not right. So if you back away from those men and come over here and I will take you to a place where you can catch a train tonight. So he drove me from Fayetteville to a place called Aberdeen, North Carolina, and saw that I got to the train station and he said the train leaves out of here at nine going to Washington, D.C. and you can get it and I thanked him and I did but the train he put me on stopped in people's backyards and let off people. I know I left there at nine and got to Washington at ten Sunday morning. I don't know I learned a lot from that, and I came back in September in 1946 and I had time which they called terminal leave.

Phillips: Yes.

Beamer: And that meant that my discharge didn't run out till November so I still had hospital privileges, anything like that up till November. I was still in the Army; then after that I did a little work around Winchester and then I went to work in Front Royal at the old Viscose Corporation and there is another place where they had colored water fountains and white water fountains. That ended after a while; I think that ended before the 60s when a lot of stuff was going on but I stayed there till '52. They laid off a bunch of people—the company was going to be sold to another outfit —they laid me off Christmas Eve 1952 and I had that time two children and I went to a place ahh, the brick kiln [Shenandoah Brick and Tile Corp.] that was out on Smithfield Avenue run by a man named Seymour Barr. I worked there for awhile but was no benefits; you could work 100 hr. a week and you would get paid $.75 an hour. I left from Viscose making $1.56 back then which was double what I could make in Winchester and then he had a bus—Middletown, Strasburg and up and around down on [Rt.] 55 and come bring people into work and, ahh, so I did that for, ahh, six years until I got laid off. Then I went to work for National Fruit, ahh, in '54 and then I retired from there in 1990 after 37 years.

Phillips: Did you get to use the G.I. Bill in any way?

Beamer: No I didn't get to use the G.I. Bill. I had, when I went into the Army, go in with a group of fellows and I put my age up a month so on my discharge it would be different then.

Phillips: Your certificate?

Beamer: Yeah, so I didn't know I never checked. Because I wasn't doing anything I never checked to see if that would matter that much. I don't know, I meant since I have been in the V.F.W., I've been intending to check it when I bought my house. I didn't have to go through the G.I. Bill. I was lucky to be able to buy my house and then, far as I haven't even been able to use the hospital benefits. All the fellows told me that I better go get my medication and stuff like that. I have had bypass surgery and I got good doctors over here which I don't want to change then I would like to keep what I got.

Phillips: What rank did you have when you got released?

Beamer: I was T5, technician fifth grade they called it. When I came out I have that rank. All the time it was hard to get any rank over there at that time.

Phillips: Did you stay in the Reserves or anything like that?

Beamer: No. They kept us in Fort Bragg trying to get us to re-enlist because we weren't regular Army or anything. I had seen plenty and I was lucky to get back and been through a lot and I didn't want to go through that again.

Phillips: Do you think the time you spent in the military was any value to you?

Beamer: Yes. I met a lot of people; I wish I could remember who they were; I don't remember their names. I kept contact with some after but either they died out or I never wrote, and then like I was telling you that I had good officers. I had really, had good officers, I can't complain about that, All the officers were white but it is like anything you have, I suppose that is the way they grew up. When we were first out there, they said don't salute the officers when you were out in the jungle. So when we got back, we had what we called shavetails, second lieutenants, thirty-day wonders or whatever you wanted to call them, and we would say to them if you don't act right we are going to salute you when we get out there, but nothing ever happened. I won't say I would do it again but I enjoyed it when I was out there. I enjoyed the people and other than a few small things for that time, I don't think I ran into that many problems.

Phillips: Were any of your children in the military?

Beamer: My son was in Vietnam, my oldest; my other son was in the Air Force. He didn't like it; he didn't stay in but a year then he came out.

Phillips: Did you ever talk to your son that was in Vietnam and compare experiences?

Beamer: Their experience was a little bit different than mine like they were in I think some tank outfit. Well they were all mixed up in that group; when they went out they went out like that now compared to where I was. I never saw a black tank group in the Philippines. I know there were some but I never saw them.

Phillips: I think there were some in Italy.

Beamer: Yes, some in Italy because they had the Ninety-second Infantry in Italy. I think I never saw any of them but at that time it was little hotter in Vietnam than we ran into at the time. The Philippines had, we had like three armies in the Philippines—you had the American white army, you had the Philippine army, and then you had the black troops in the Philippine army—so you had to go along with whatever rules they had there and we didn't come into much contact with them. We kind of kept away from them and we couldn't carry any weapons. I think all of them carried weapons. When we first got there we didn't carry weapons that any one knew about but there where plenty of people who carried weapons if they wanted to. After that I can't think of much more that went on. I got married after that and had four children and been married this past November 55 years so I guess I have had a good life.

Phillips: Is there anything else that you would like to add?

Beamer: No I think that about covered it.

Phillips: Well Mr. Beamer, I thank you very much.

Beamer: Well, I thank you for listening.

Beamer, Phillips: hahahaha.

Tom Laws

Tom Laws: The Life and Times of General Sheridan's Messenger

William H. Austin

It was September 16, 1864. A very brave slave living in Clarke County, Virginia, named Tom Laws delivered vital communications through Confederate lines between Union General Philip Sheridan and a 26-year-old Quaker schoolteacher, Rebecca Wright in Winchester, Virginia.[1] After being contacted by Union scouts, he was subsequently asked by Sheridan to carry a foil-wrapped message in his mouth to and from Miss Wright. It would be an event that changed people's lives forever as well as the course of Civil War history in the Shenandoah Valley.

Sheridan was near Berryville, Virginia, with some 40,000 troops preparing to engage Confederate General Jubal Early and his troops in Winchester. Sheridan needed additional intelligence on the numbers and placement of Early's army. Sheridan reports in his 1888 memoir that "I knew I was strong, yet, in consequence of the injunctions of General Grant, I deemed it necessary to be very cautious; and the fact that the presidential election was impending made me doubly so."[2] Despite his superior strength, Sheridan set about to gather the fullest information possible to assure success. Two Union scouts reported that Tom Laws, near Millwood, had a permit from the Confederate commander to go to Winchester and return three times a week to sell vegetables. They found him "both loyal and shrewd." Their interview also revealed his master, Richard E. Byrd, was provost marshal in Winchester.[3] Meanwhile, General George Crook, who knew many civilians in Winchester with Union sentiments, recommended Rebecca Wright as a faithful person of Union loyalty who might give information on Confederate forces.[4]

Laws was taken to the Mount Pope farm near Sheridan's headquarters at Mannsfield on Monday night, September 12.[5] The two sat on an old log as Sheridan asked Laws if he knew Rebecca Wright and Laws said he did not, but that he thought he could find her. Sheridan completed the interview and then ultimately decided to ask Laws to be his messenger. On September 15, he prepared a letter for Rebecca that read in part: "I learn from Major General

Crook that you are a Loyal Lady and still love the Old Flag." Then Sheridan asked for information about the number of men Early had and whether more were coming from Richmond. He ended the note with, "You can trust the bearer."[6]

Sheridan wrote his message on tissue paper compressed into a small pellet and wrapped in tinfoil. Laws was instructed to carry the packet in his mouth and swallow it if he were searched by Confederate troops. On September 16, 1864, Laws set out on his mission and with the help of slave Matilda Robinson, "a woman raised in the yard with my wife," he found Miss Wright.[7] Laws asked to speak with Miss Wright. Rebecca responded that she was Miss Wright but that she also had a sister.

"Perhaps thee wants to see my sister Hannah," said Rebecca. "No, I don't," replied Laws. "Your sister is not on our side, I want to see Miss Wright the Unionist. I have a letter for her from General Sheridan." Laws took the concealed note from his mouth and while giving it to her warned not to damage the foil, because he would be carrying her response back through Confederate lines just as he had brought it in. He then announced that he would return for her reply that afternoon at 3 p.m.[8]

Wright initially thought perhaps Tom Laws' visit was a Confederate ploy to trap her, as they were then in possession of the town. After discussing the matter with her mother and despite concerns of possible discovery, at great personal risk to herself and family, she responded to Sheridan; "I have no communications whatever with the rebels, but will tell you what I know. The divisions of General Kershaw, Artillery, 12 guns and men, General Anderson commanding, have been sent away and no more are expected as they cannot be spared from Richmond. I do not know how the troops are situated but the force is smaller than represented."[9]

Tom Laws retrieved her response and returned through Confederate lines to his cabin where scout James A. Campbell[e], Co. A, 2nd New York Cavalry was waiting to deliver the message to Sheridan that night.[10] On that same evening, General William Averell sent Sheridan a dispatch that confirmed Anderson's departure. Sheridan also learned that General Grant wanted to see him in Charles Town, so he deferred action until he could meet with his commander.

When the generals met on September 17, Grant was so impressed with Sheridan's battle plan that he simply ordered him to "go in." Grant had brought a battle plan as well, but concluded that Sheridan "was so clear and so positive in his views and so confident of success, I said nothing about this and did not take it out of my pocket."[11]

Rebecca Wright wondered over the next two days whether her message had reached Sheridan. She finally got her answer on the third day, September 19, following the Third Battle of Winchester, when General Sheridan, himself, came to her porch. She later recalled, "He told me it was entirely on the information I had sent him that he fought the battle. I begged him not to mention it, as my life would not be safe when our troops went away. 'Oh,' he said, 'The rebels will never come again.' "[12]

It could be said that between the efforts of Tom Laws and Rebecca Wright, General Sheridan was able to confirm valuable information needed to launch the Third Battle of Winchester and ultimately gain control of the valley for the remainder of the war. Of course, were either Laws or Wright found out for their efforts, it would mean almost certain death. Still, Laws followed through. A great deal is known about how this unlikely pair's role in support of the Union changed Miss Wright's life forever.

Rebecca Wright: The Informant

The Civil War wounded and divided Rebecca Wright's family. Her decision to help Sheridan was undoubtedly driven in part by the 1861 arrest and imprisonment of her fervent Unionist father by Confederate authorities and the conscription of a brother forced to serve a cause he opposed.

Sheridan's personal gratitude toward Wright is well known. Rebecca appears to have lived quietly with her mother in Winchester until January 1867, when Sheridan sent her a letter personally delivered by General James Forsyth, again thanking her, and enclosing a gift of a watch and chain. "You are not probably aware of how great a service you rendered the Union cause,"[13] he wrote.

Soon after, Rebecca's sister, Hannah, apparently revealed the entire story behind the new watch and chain to a Baltimore newspaper reporter. When the story was reprinted in Winchester, Rebecca suffered great disdain from fellow citizens as a traitor to the South. After months of torment, she finally wrote Sheridan of her trouble; who, in turn, asked General Grant for help. On July 6, 1868, Rebecca Wright was appointed to the post of clerk at U.S. Treasury Department.[14] She moved to Washington, D.C., where she lived the rest of her life. Rebecca married William C. Bonsal in 1871 and continued at her Treasury post until 1910. She died May 15, 1914, and is buried in Glenwood Cemetery, in Washington, D.C.[15]

Thomas Laws: the Messenger

Tom's story, perhaps not surprisingly, appears to have been nearly forgotten. After all, he had been a slave and lived through a time when blacks were trying to assimilate into a newly defined southern culture. At war's end he most certainly would not have wished to publicly discuss his own role in helping to bring about the Third Battle of Winchester, nor would anyone else who cared about his safety do so. This is the story of Tom Laws—a slave, Union patriot, farmer, and family man.

The only known first-person account of Tom Laws' role as Sheridan's messenger was first published in *The James E. Taylor Sketchbook* (1900) in response to Taylor's inquiry. Tom Laws responded with a letter dated Sept. 26, 1894, transcribed as follows:

Mr. Taylor, Dear Sir:
Yours to hand, would say in reply that I'll send you my photo with much pleasure and also a short history of the facts connected with my trip to Winchester and how I came to go, ec. [sic]

I was borned and raised in Clarke County, Virginia, and was owned by Richard Bird [Byrd]. My age is between 75 and 80 years, I married a woman belonging to Old Mr. Philip Burrill [Burwell]. She and I were sitting on the steps one Sunday evening. Two unknown men came through the yard and struck up a conversation with me about Winchester. I told them I could go to Winchester any time I chooses as my master lived there, that was, in Berryville, Sunday night, Sept. 11, and on Monday night these same two came back to my house and said to me, "The general wants to see you tonight."

I got ready and started right off with them to the headquarters. They carried me to the general. When I got there, the general and I took our seat on an old log that was laying by the camp, and he asked me could I go to Winchester tomorrow, and I told him I could go there anytime the Rebels were there for my master lived there, and then the general asked me, did I know Miss Rebecca Wright. I told him I did not but I had a great many acquaintances in Winchester, I could find out. So I went to a lady, which was raised in the yard with my wife which I married, Matilda Robinson, telling her my errand. She quickly pointed me [to] the house. I went to the front door and knocked and Mrs. Wright came to the door and I asked, "Could I see Miss Rebecca Wright" and she called her to the door. I asked Miss Rebecca, "Could I see her privately." She went into the school room in which she was teachin. I asked her, "Was she a Union lady," she said she was. I asked her then, "did she know the general?" She said she did not and when she said she did not, I thought I was between Heaven and Earth. I ventured anyhow and gave her the letter which was sent to her and in the afternoon I called and got her reply and gave it to the scouts that night.

Yours truly, Thomas Laws,
September 26, 1894[16]

Neither Tom nor Mary Laws reportedly could read or write according to the 1870 and 1880 U.S. Census reports. The 1890 Census was lost in a fire, so we cannot know if he was literate at that time. So perhaps Tom learned to read and write in the intervening 14 years or one of his children or grandchildren may have penned the letter as he dictated. Nevertheless, we have no reason to question its authenticity.

Born and Raised a Slave

Thomas Laws was born in Clarke County, Virginia, on January 7, 1817.[17] Thomas' master, Richard Evelyn Byrd was born in 1801 to Captain Thomas Taylor and Mary Armistead Byrd at the family home called The Cottage.[18] It was Captain (a British army officer) Thomas Taylor Byrd who acquired 1,008 acres of Frederick County land in 1790,[19] now in Clarke County, northwest of Old Chapel Church. The Byrds' original home, The Cottage was located near Lewis spring.[20] Byrd's land would have extended southward from about Senseny Road, in proximity of modern U.S. 340, to beyond Old Chapel Church and cemetery.

Upon his death on August 19, 1821, Captain Byrd's "estate of every kind, both real and personal" passed to his wife Mary.[21] According to a "family friendly" Bill of Complaint, filed January 3, 1825, Thomas Taylor Sr. had verbally instructed that his real property be divided equally among the Byrd children; sons Thomas Taylor Jr., Charles Carter, Francis Otway, Richard Evelyn and daughters Maria Carter (Nicholas) and Elizabeth Hill Byrd. Mary Byrd had distributed properties to the children during her lifetime, but had not been able to fully comply with her husband's wishes by the time of her death.[22] Court appointed commissioners returned a report dated October 22, 1825, which enabled fair and equal distribution of lands as requested in the lawsuit.[23]

A slave child, Thomas was first mentioned in Mary Byrd's will signed March 6, 1824,[24] probated December 6, 1824. "My son Charles Carter Byrd is to be allowed to take [slave] Nancy's son Thomas as one of his share if he wishes to have him & son Richard Evelyn is also to be permitted to make choice of Nancy's daughter Nancy as one of his share of my slaves."[25]

Nancy and her three children appear on Mary's estate inventory recorded January 2, 1826.[26] Mary's account summaries do not reveal what happened to Nancy.[27] Could Nancy's son Thomas be Thomas Laws at 7 years old?[28] If this was Thomas Laws, he was not the only male slave with the surname Laws at the Mary Byrd estate. William Laws, age 15, appears on her account of appraisement.[29] Wellington Laws is found in a conveyance of property deed executed October 1, 1824, between the Byrd children. That entry identifies slaves "George Potter White & Eppy Laws (called Wellington) conveyed in trust by said late Mary A. Byrd."[30]

Dr. Charles Carter Byrd built a house known as Chapel Hill during 1825–26 on his 168-acre portion (plus four acres previously acquired) of his parents' estate.[31] Chapel Hill is located near Old Chapel on the west side of today's U.S. 340 near the Bishop Meade Road intersection on Chapel Hill Lane.[32] No sooner was Chapel Hill finished than it was sold to Philip Burwell on a deed signed November 27, 1826, which described Dr. and Mrs. Byrd as "formerly of Frederick County, Va. but now of Montgomery County, Md."[33] Dr. Byrd died December 14, 1829, at the age of 30, a scarce three years later.[34]

Typically, slaves remained property of an estate until the estate formally closed—even those noted in a will as bequeathed freedom or distribution to an heir. As executor for both the Thomas T. Byrd and Mary A. Byrd estates, Richard E. Byrd filed four settlement accounts from April 1827 through January 1835. In the 1835 settlement account, Mary Byrd's December 25, 1829, entry lists fees paid to the estate for the hiring out of slaves during that year. Among them was Tom Laws who garnered the estate five dollars for his services.[35] He would have been about age 12 at the time. So, as of December 1829, this Thomas Laws was still the property of Mary A. Byrd's estate.

Evidence to date shows that Charles C. Byrd never took possession of Nancy's son Thomas.[36] Furthermore, we have not yet established that Thomas willed to Charles, is the same Thomas Laws found on Mary's settlement account—although Thomas Laws' known birth year and age during these events would make it entirely plausible they are one and the same person.

Exactly how and when Richard Evelyn Byrd acquired Thomas Laws is still unknown at this writing, but he undoubtedly would have had many opportunities to do so as attorney and executor for both parents' estates.

The 1840 U.S. Census shows Richard E. Byrd owned six slaves and housed a free colored person in Frederick County and owned one male slave older than Laws in Clarke County.[37] A Thomas Laws was listed on Clarke County's personal property tax lists as a free black in 1840.[38] An annual poll tax was paid to the county on all free black and white adult males at that time. No tax was paid in 1840 and Tom Laws never appeared on any subsequent Clarke County personal property tax roll through 1862. No tax rolls exist for 1863 and 1864. If he were briefly freed, no emancipation deed or certificate of emancipation was found. We can only surmise that he returned to slave status.

Philip Burwell, during his lifetime, "improved the gardens and grounds around Chapel Hill and brought the estate up to a high degree of cultivation; it is with this owner the home is most frequently associated."[39] Tom Laws tells us he "married a woman that belonged to Old Phil Burrill [Burwell]" and we know from later census records her name to be Mary. He also tells us his wife and her friend Matilda Robinson, his contact point in Winchester, "grew up together in the yard." Could he be referring to the yard of Chapel Hill?

In 1842, Phil Burwell was taxed for three slaves between 12 and 16 years of age and 27 slaves over 16 years of age in Clarke County.[40] Upon Burwell's death on February 11, 1849, an estate inventory dated February 26, 1849, listed 68 Negroes valued at $19,000. Among them were two slave women named Mary. One Mary was with child, valued at $450 and devised to Mrs. Burwell for her lifetime while the other was not devised and valued at $350. Two children listed immediately below the second Mary's entry were valued at $350.[41] Mary Laws would have been about age 25 at the time. Could either of Mrs. Burwell's slaves named Mary be Mary Laws?

Clarke County personal property tax records of 1842 show one slave older than age 16 and one horse or mule listed for the "T.T. Byrd Est."[42] In 1850 there was one slave over age 16 and two horses or mules listed.[43] This was the estate of T.T. Byrd Jr. who died sometime before May 1842. His brother, executor Richard E. Byrd managed the estate until May 1851.[44] Could this slave have been Laws? Thomas Laws would have been about 25 years of age in 1842 and about 33 years of age in 1850. A review of the 1850 U.S. Slave Schedules shows Richard E. Byrd of Frederick County Virginia, District 16, recorded seven slaves under his control; those of his own plus any hired away from others in accordance with 1850 Census policy.[45]

Slave marriage records do not exist, but Tom and Mary Laws' first-born son, Charles, arrived about 1850 or 1851.[46] Exactly where Tom and Mary Laws lived is not certain, but, they were likely quartered separately on the Byrd and Burwell estates near Old Chapel. Typical Clarke County slave quarters housed as many as 10 persons in extremely crowded, communal conditions. Many of them had patches of ground for gardens and slave families were often allowed to have a hog or a hen house for chickens.[47]
A four-room stone slave cabin stood at the time near Chapel Hill

on the approximate centerline of modern U.S. 340.[48] This particular structure probably housed a mix of families as space allowed—not necessarily as complete family units within each room.

Clarke County personal property tax rolls for each year from 1854 through 1856 show one slave and one horse belonging to Richard E. Byrd.[49] Mr. Byrd owned 26 slaves according to the 1860 U.S. Slave Census Schedule.[50] By now, all of Byrd's slaves were listed in Frederick County. Only slaves' age, sex and color were noted, but just one individual, a 44-year-old male would have been about the same age and mulatto complexion we now know Tom Laws to have been.[51]

The Civil War Years

Phil Burwell's widow, Susan R. Burwell, continued to live at Chapel Hill until the outbreak of the Civil War whereupon she relocated just down the road to the New Market estate under the protection of her son-in-law, Dr. Robert C. Randolph. Mrs. Burwell would have continued to oversee Chapel Hill throughout the war since the two properties were in close proximity and her slaves would have been readily available to her at either location. This circumstance could help explain why at least one slave named Mary was still living in the area in 1864. Mrs. Burwell died in Clarke County on December 27, 1869, and Chapel Hill was sold at public auction on October 28, 1870.[52]

We can be reasonably assured that when Union scouts called in September 1864, Tom Laws was found in approximately the same area where he had always been; probably living in a cabin he did not own with or near his own growing family. Thomas would have been about 47 and Mary, 40 years old, with four children–two boys and two girls.

Richard Byrd, a prominent attorney throughout his career, served the Confederacy from his Winchester offices. Just as Tom Laws said, Mr. Byrd was Winchester's Provost Marshal. He was staff officer to General James H. Carson, commander of the Militia Brigade. General Thomas Jackson appointed him to that post in November 1861 with commission as colonel.[53] Captain John B. Neal, 1st North Carolina Cavalry purchased 230¾ bushels of corn from Byrd on a $300 note dated October 20, 1862. The note was paid on June 14, 1864, by a Captain Dorsey.[54]

A January 20, 1863, letter to Maj. Gen. Robert C. Schenck from C. Dewitt Smith written on behalf of Richard E. Byrd, requests authority to provide supplies to Byrd's Winchester family. Mr. Byrd was at the time imprisoned in Baltimore for assisting Smith, himself previously accused as a spy and imprisoned. Mr. Byrd had worked to secure Smith's release.[55] During that same year, Byrd was stricken with paralysis from which he never recovered.[56] At war's end, he was excluded from earlier amnesty proclamations and thus formally received his pardon from President Andrew Johnson on July 5, 1866.[57] R. E. Byrd remained an invalid until his death on January 1, 1872, and is buried at Old Chapel Church Cemetery.

A New Beginning

Events happened quickly at war's end in April 1865. Winchester's Bureau of Refugees, Freedmen and Abandoned Lands office opened in 1866. As noted in the *Final Report, African-American Historic Context, Clarke County, VA*, the bureau's purpose was to benefit all blacks, "to insure good health, sustenance, and legal rights, to make negroes self-supporting, and to provide the 'foundation of education' for all."[58] Ratification of the 13th Amendment outlawed slavery and the 14th promised all people equal protection under the law and rights of citizenship. Virginia was under close supervision of military commanders from 1867 until January 1870.[59]

The Reconstruction Era

Clarke County postwar 1867 personal property tax records list Tom Laws' residence at Chapel Hill.[60] A former Confederate officer on General Jubal Early's staff, Major Samuel J.C. Moore, (also known as a respected local attorney and mayor of Berryville) claims to have employed Tom Laws as gardener in 1869 and to have asked him about his role in delivering General Sheridan's message to Miss Wright.

"At first he was not inclined to talk about it, but upon my assuring him that I would not hurt him, I got him to talk freely about it" he said. Moore reports that Tom said he was promised $50 for carrying the message, but that he never got the money.[61] This account is the only known claim where money is involved. Would a shrewd Tom Laws tell such a story to a former Confederate soldier to illustrate a slave's reasonable justification—for the benefit of his listener? In truth, Laws' readiness to help no doubt most probably had less to do with a reward than with a hope to speed emancipation for all.

Former slave owners often struggled to keep their farms without free black labor forces. Former slaves typically worked the same type of jobs as before and during the Civil War, but for wages or sharing the proceeds of the crop.[62] Thomas Laws appears on the 1868 Clarke County personal property tax rolls at Mrs. Kownslar's farm and again in 1869 as "Laws & Son, Thomas."[63] It just so happens that former Confederate officer Samuel J.C. Moore, who had asked Thomas about his role in delivering Sheridan's message, was related through marriage to the Kownslar family.[64]

On a Deed of Bargain and Sale dated December 14, 1869, Robert Hall and his wife sold one-half acre of land "beginning on the Berryville and Charlestown Turnpike, corner, to Henry Slow, thence with his line" to trustees of the African Methodist Episcopal Church "to be built thereon a house or place of worship." Thomas Laws was among seven trustees executing this church property purchase.[65] This old church building still stands at 208 N. Buckmarsh Street, Berryville, along with a few cemetery headstones and stone fragment.

The 1870 U.S. census enumerates Tom Laws, age 53, living in Clarke County, Battletown Township, with Mary and five children. Both Tom and son Charles "works on farm," and the rest of the family are, "wife Mary 50, Charles 15, Kit [Thomas Jr.] 13, Martha A. 11, Nancy F. 9, Mary J. 2; James Champ 37."[66]

A prominent white family, the Kownslar household, appears on the same 1870 Census page as the Laws family where multiple other black and white neighbors are shown to be domestic servants or farm laborers. At the time, widow Elizabeth Kownslar was still operating her 117-acre farm Ambrosia.[67] She owned $13,000 in real estate, held $27,000 in personal property and may have employed these neighbors.

Typically farm laborers of the period were housed on the farms they worked and census-takers listed all owners, renters, and sharecroppers as separate households. Tax rolls of 1870 show that Mrs. Kownslar owned six horses or mules. Ambrosia, acquired by Dr. Randolph Kownslar in 1853, was located along modern U.S. 340, in Battletown Township, about one mile north of today's Berryville.[70]

On July 22, 1874, Elizabeth S. Kownslar sold Ambrosia consisting of about 117 acres to her first son, Randolph Kownslar. It was originally conveyed by J. Samuel Taylor and Elizabeth T., his wife, on April 8, 1853, to Dr. Randolph Kownslar; and willed to Elizabeth Kownslar by Dr. Randolph Kownslar, deceased.[71] The Ambrosia dwelling was torn down in the summer of 1974.[72]

Economic realities and Virginia's Jim Crow laws, combined with its Reconstruction-era black codes, greatly affected how black communities, schools, churches, and services evolved. On September 19, 1870, Tom Laws purchased a lot offered at public auction by Clermont Farm owner Ellen S. McCormick, executor for Edward McCormick, deceased.

The land became Josephine City, a 31-acre village on the southern outskirts of Berryville. Mrs. McCormick kept the timber rights and specified that a new street be established for the common good.[73] Tom Laws purchased Lot #5 on the south side of the road. Some buyers, including Laws, agreed to a vendor's lien on the purchase price of $100 per lot at 6 percent interest.

He must have found it very difficult to make loan payments while providing for his family as a wage earner or sharecropper. Although we do not currently know Reconstruction-era black wages in Clarke County, some Southern black farm worker's wages in 1867 were estimated to have been from $100 to $158 per year.

For sharecroppers, typically a landlord furnished a stipulated sum of money payable in monthly installments until the crop was "laid by." In lieu of money, landlords might even arrange with a time merchant to furnish the cropper provisions within certain limits.[74]

In the Upper South, black laborers were able to supplement wages earned on farms by working small plots of land they were able to purchase.[75]

By 1875, 10 black communities were in various stages of development in Clarke County and the Laws family seemed to be making progress; still farming and in need of equipment. Tom Laws purchased a wagon bed for $3.95 and a wheat drill for $29 at the Edward W. Massey estate sale on May 22, 1876[76] and one heifer for $20 at the William D. McGuire estate sale on May 2, 1878.[77]

On October 16, 1878, Thomas Laws Jr, age 25, second son of Tom and Mary, married Bettie Jenkins, age 23 in Berryville. Both were black and born and raised in Clarke County. Thomas was a farmhand.[78]

On November 8, 1879, Tom Laws was named defendant in a lawsuit brought by Elizabeth McCormick for $76.33 plus 6 percent interest due on his one-acre Josephine lot purchased in the fall of 1870, now in default. He was ordered to make full payment within 30 days or to forfeit the property. If not paid, Sheriff John T. Crow was to take possession and sell the lot at public auction to settle the debt with time, place, and terms fixed by publication in the *Clarke Courier* newspaper.[79]

As a result of a chancery cause, Thomas Laws' Lot #5 in Josephine City was sold on January 30, 1882, by Sheriff Crow to Trustees of Battletown School District "for the purposes of building a public school house thereon."[80] A *Clarke Courier* advertisement, June 15, 1882, asked for "sealed proposals to build a school house . . . .The building, we understand, will be erected in the settlement known as Josephine city, which is inhabited by colored people." Josephine School opened in the fall of that same year.[81] Josephine School was moved to its current location from its original building site in 1930. It is now the Josephine Community School Museum dedicated to telling the Josephine City story.

By the summer of 1880, Tom, Mary and their family were still living in Battletown Township on or near the Kownslar family's Ambrosia farm. The 1880 census described the Laws family: "Clarke County Virginia, Page 18, Dwelling 110: Thomas Laws,

Mulatto, age 63, Farmer, wife Mary 56, Charles 29, Thomas Jr. 26, Martha A. 23, Nancy 19, Mary J. 11."[82]   One could argue about the difference between the census designation terms "farmer" in the 1880 census and "works on farm" from the 1870 counting. Perhaps this was an attempt to imply that Tom might own land as opposed to simply working for someone else. The only property he ever owned, however, was lost within Josephine City.

On April 6 or 7, 1881 Charles Laws, age 30, the first son of Tom and Mary married Mary McCard, age 21, in Berryville. Both were noted as black and born and raised in Clarke County. Charles was a farmhand and the marriage license notes Tom and Mary Laws as the husband's parents.[83]

Mary Laws died on July 11, 1885 at the approximate age of 61.[84] Now without Mary and even at an advanced age, Tom Laws continued to need farm equipment. He purchased a lunge frame for $10 at the James H. Vandevanter estate sale on January 4, 1887.[85]

Union Veterans Come Calling

A history of the 23rd Pennsylvania Volunteer Infantry mentions that survivors of the Sixth Corps dedicated a monument to General David A. Russell at Winchester in September 1891. "Up to the year 1891, the colored man that carried the dispatch, had not been found, although every effort had been made to find him" it reports. Found in Berryville, Tom Laws was transported to Washington D.C., where he was identified by Mrs. Bonsal (Rebecca Wright).[86]

Bonsal gave her affidavit of identity at the War Department, "which is now on file." The entry continues, "At this time the faithful messenger was 78 years of age, never lived in a city, and while a position was offered him for the balance of his life, he refused, as he was then living with his grandchildren and doing well and contented."[87]   The veterans incorrectly state he had been owned by a Mr. Clarke who resided in Winchester at the time of the war. In fact, we now know that Tom Laws was owned by Richard E. Byrd of Winchester.

The Legacy of Tom Laws

Tom Laws as slave, farmer, and family man turned patriot helped bring about the bloodiest and most significant Civil War battle in the Shenandoah Valley and Union control of the valley for the remainder of the war. Indeed, he was a courageous man. But perhaps his greatest legacy was living through Reconstruction to see his own children and grandchildren make their own way in the adversity and opportunities of a changing society. Tom Laws died at the age of 79 on April 16, 1896. He is buried along with his wife Mary under a cedar tree in Milton Valley Cemetery, Berryville. Their tombstone was put in place by C. Laws (Charles H. Laws.)[88]

Tom Laws tombstone. Milton Valley Cemetery Berryville, Virginia

Charles Laws, first son of Tom and Mary, continued living and working in Berryville for the remainder of his life. In 1883, Charles was one of several Trustees of Lodge Twenty-Four of the order of the brothers and sisters of Love and Charity of Clarke County.[89] The 1900 U.S. Census lists him as a head of household, married 19 years, with eight children, working as a teamster. That census lists the children of Charles Laws and Mary McCard as follows:

Charles A. Laws, born abt 1881 in Virginia
Joseph H. Laws, born abt 1883 in Virginia
Benjamin T. Laws, born abt 1885 in Virginia
Sadie M. Laws, born abt 1887 in Virginia
Emma R. Laws, born abt 1889 in Virginia
William G. Laws, born abt 1891 in Virginia
Nathan B. Laws, born abt 1893 in Virginia
Lander H. Laws, born abt 1895 in Virginia[90]

Charles Laws is found in the 1910 U.S. Census for Clarke County as head of household, with wife Mary A. and children Willie, Nathaniel, and Leander living in Berryville, Ward 1.[91] By the 1920 U.S. Census, Charles was 68, married to Mary A., and worked as a laborer in the coal yard. He owned a home on Liberty Street, a traditionally black neighborhood in the northeast quadrant of Berryville often referred to as Blackburn Town.[92]

Charles died September 24, 1925, and is buried along with other family members in Milton Valley Cemetery. His death certificate informant was a daughter, Sadie Laws of Chicago.[93] Sadie Laws, age 32, appears in the 1920 U.S. Census at East 36th Street, Chicago, as a lodger, working as a seamstress.[94] A bronze marker at the entrance of Milton Valley Cemetery notes that Charles Laws and Thomas Laws Jr. were original stockholders when the cemetery was established in 1874.

Unfortunately, we'll probably never know as much about Thomas Laws as we would like, but his story as told to James Taylor in 1894 meshes well with the bits-and-pieces of the historical record we do know.

Tom Laws' life was probably simple by most standards of his time, but it was also extremely significant in so many ways. He grew up a slave and was occupied with selling vegetables when Sheridan's scouts came calling. Chapel Hill, where his wife was enslaved, still stands today near Old Chapel Church and the village of Millwood.

It is in this proximity and on nearby lands, in a community of slaves where he lived, grew to manhood, married, and met the challenges of his time and place. Tom and Mary Laws must have sacrificed greatly and worked hard to meet their family's needs, particularly during the Civil War. Tom Laws was probably a trusted slave in late 1864; but, if not a slave, he certainly would have known slavery all around him.

General Sheridan's purpose in asking this African American man to carry his message through enemy lines was motivated for reasons of great strategic importance to the Union, but Tom Laws likely put himself at risk simply to gain a better life for himself and his family. Certainly, a brighter future and better life for the people living behind his cabin door that day in 1864 was made possible, in part, because of his brave, unselfish act. Indeed, he must have been shrewd to remain mostly anonymous to outsiders while continuing to live among his Clarke County neighbors as "a respectable negro." Rebecca Wright later wrote of Mr. Laws, "I found him a quiet, dignified, sensible colored man."[95] And so it was—she has undoubtedly been proven absolutely correct.

28

ENDNOTES

---

[1] 1860 U.S. Census, database and images, *Ancestry.com*
(http://www.ancestry.com: accessed Feb. 15, 2016), entry for Rebecca L.
Wright, Winchester, Frederick County, Virginia. p. 111; Wright was age 22 in
1860, therefore age 26 in 1864.

[2] Philip H. Sheridan, *Personal Memoirs of P.H. Sheridan* (New York: Charles L.
Webster, 1888), 1: 499-500.

[3] James E. Taylor, *The James E. Taylor Sketchbook* (Dayton: Morningside
House, 1989), 350; Thomas D. Gold, *History of Clarke County Virginia and Its
Connection with the War Between the States* (Berryville: Chesapeake Book,
1962), 121.

[4] Philip H. Sheridan, *Personal Memoirs of P.H. Sheridan* (New York: Charles L.
Webster, 1888), 2: 3.

[5] Taylor, Taylor Sketchbook, map, 349; Lorraine Meyers and Stuart E. Brown,
Jr., Annals of Clarke County Virginia, (Berryville: Virginia Book, 2002), 4:
155. Sheridan headquartered here, while the Union line ran from Clifton to
Berryville.

[6] Taylor, Taylor Sketchbook, 350–55; Sheridan, Personal Memoirs, 2: 5–6.

[7] Taylor, *Taylor Sketchbook*, 355.

[8] Sylvia G. L. Dannett, "Rebecca Wright–Traitor or Patriot," *Lincoln Herald*
(1963) vol., 65, no 3, 103–106, Lincoln Memorial University Press, Harrogate,
Tennessee.

[9] Taylor, *Taylor Sketchbook*, 350–55.

[10] Sheridan, *Personal Memoirs*, 2: 3–4; Letter of Arch Rowand, Sheridan's
Scouts, to War Department, Sept. 3, 1897, National Archives.

[11] Scott Patchan, *The Last Battle of Winchester* (El Dorado Hills, Calif.: Savas
Beatie, 2013), 193–94.

[12] Dannett, "Rebecca Wright—Traitor or Patriot," 108–110.

[13] Ibid, 110.

[14] Jonathan A. Noyalas, *Civil War Legacy in the Shenandoah*, (Charleston: The
History Press, 2015) 29–32; United States Treasury Register, 41.

[15] Dannett, "Rebecca Wright—Traitor or Patriot." 110–12.

[16] Taylor, *Taylor Sketchbook*, 355.

[17] Milton Valley Cemetery (Berryville, Clarke County, Virginia); Thomas Laws
marker, plot W-E-28; personal observation, 2017; Taylor, *Taylor Sketchbook*,
355. Tom Laws' letter says he was born and raised in Clarke County.
The Find A Grave Memorial database, Find A Grave,
http://www.findagrave.com, entry for Thomas Laws, Berryville, Clarke County,
Virginia, lists June 17, 1817, as Thomas Laws' birth date and does not reflect the
actual date January 7, 1817, engraved on the headstone. The author will

consistently cite January 7, 1817, as the true birth date for Thomas Laws.

[18] Myers and Brown, *Annals of Clarke County Virginia*, 4: 111; Charles Randolph Hughes, *"Old Chapel," Clarke County, Virginia* (Berryville: The Blue Ridge Press, 1906), 48.

[19] Mary G. Farland and Beverly B. Byrd, *In the Shadow of the Blue Ridge: Clarke County 1732–1952* (Richmond: William Byrd Press, 1978), 74.

[20] Myers and Brown, *Annals of Clarke*, 4: 111.

[21] Frederick County, Virginia, Will Book 11: 436. (dtd Aug. 6, 1821, rec May 2, 1823).

[22] Frederick County, Virginia Chancery Record: microfilm reel 222. Image 226. Bill of Complaint filed in 1825, Philip Norborne Nicholas, Maria his wife and Eliz Hill Byrd vs. Francis O. Byrd et als.

[23] Richard E. Griffith, "Early Estates of Clarke County," Clarke County Historical Association (Boyce: Carr Publishing, 1954), 11–12: 9-10.

[24] Frederick County, Virginia, Will Book 12: 175. (dtd March 6, 1824, prob Dec. 6, 1824).

[25] Ibid, 175.

[26] Frederick County, Virginia, Will Book, 13: 96.

[27] Frederick County, Virginia, Will Book 13: 477; 15: 388; 18: 480.

[28] Laws marker, plot W-E-28; personal observation, 2017. Marker shows birth date of January 7, 1817. Laws would have been about age 7 in 1824.

[29] Frederick County, Virginia, Will Book 13: 96.

[30] Frederick County, Virginia, Deed Book 49: 111. (dtd Oct. 1, 1824, rec Oct. 4, 1824).

[31] Griffith, *Early Estates*, 10–11.

[32] Farland and Byrd, *In the Shadow of the Blue Ridge*, 74.

[33] Frederick County, Virginia, Deed Book 52: 500. (dtd Nov. 27, 1826, rec Apr. 27, 1827).

[34] Griffith, *Early Estates*, 10–11; Byrd marker, Lot 19; personal observation, 2016. Marker shows date of death as December 14, 1829, aged 30.

[35] Frederick County, Virginia, Will Book 18: 480. (Estate Account dtd Jan. 3, 1835, rcd Jan. 5, 1835).

[36] Charles C. Byrd's will was not found, but multiple inventories, a sale bill, and various other account records regarding his Maryland estate were recorded in Montgomery County, Maryland, from early 1830 through May 1837. The administrator, David Teundle, listed six slaves in the initial estate inventory, dated Dec. 31, 1829, but a "Thomas" was not among them. (Montgomery County, Maryland, Will Book R: 58. 1828–1831. MSA C1138-20; Maryland State Archives, Annapolis) A sale bill dated Jan. 25–26, 1830, recorded March 12, 1831, shows the sale of four Negroes including a girl Sarah and a boy Joseph, purchased by Mrs. Charles Byrd, Jane F. Byrd. (Montgomery County, Maryland Will Book R: 414. 1828–1831. MSA C1138-20; Maryland State

Archives, Annapolis) Other Charles C. Byrd estate records in Montgomery County and one Frederick County, Virginia, settlement account show various Negro property transactions, but again, a "Thomas" is not listed.

[37] 1840 U.S. Census, database and images, *Ancestry.com* (http://www.ancestry.com: accessed Nov. 11, 2015), entry for Richd E. Bird (sic), Frederick County, Virginia, 50–51, line 9; Richard E. Byrd, Clarke County, 18–19, line 6.

[38] Joy MacDonald, compiler, *Free Blacks on the Personal Property Tax Lists of Clarke County Virginia 1836–1862*, (Athens Georgia: New Papyrus Publishing, 2013), 4; Marty Hiatt, *Clarke County, Virginia, Personal Property Tax Lists: 1 and 2, 1836–1870* (Berwyn Heights, Maryland: Heritage Books, 2015), 1: 48.

[39] Griffith, *Early Estates*, 11.

[40] Hiatt: *Tax Lists*, 1: 58.

[41] Clarke County, Virginia, Will Book B: 305. (Inventory and appraisement dtd Feb. 26, 1849, rec March 26, 1849).

[42] Hiatt, *Tax Lists*, 1: 59.

[43] Ibid, 141.

[44] Clarke County, Virginia, Will Book A: 262; Deed Book E: 217.

[45] 1850 U.S. Census Slave Schedule, database and images, *Ancestry.com* (http://www.ancestry.com: accessed April 11, 2016), entry for Richard E. Byrd, Winchester, Frederick County, Virginia. page 10, line 35.

[46] "1870 U.S. Census," Ancestry.com, (http://www.ancestry.com: accessed March 12, 2016), database entry for Charles Laws, Clarke County, Virginia, page 29, dwelling 178 Charles was 15 years of age.

[47] Maral S. Kalbian and Leila O.W. Boyer, *Final Report, African-American Historic Context, Clarke County, VA* (Berryville: County of Clarke, 2002), 88.

[48] Myers and Brown, *Annals of Clarke*, 4: 103.

[49] Hiatt, *Tax Lists*, 2: 2,16, 29.

[50] 1860 U.S. Slave Census, database and images, *Ancestry.com* (http://www.ancestry.com: accessed Nov. 2, 2015), entry for Richard E. Byrd, Winchester, Frederick County, Virginia. page 10, line 40.

[51] Thomas Laws' color is coded M for mulatto in the 1880 U.S Census. (1880 U.S. Census, database and images, *Ancestry.com* (http://www.ancestry.com: accessed Nov. 2, 2015), entry for Thomas Laws, Clarke County, Virginia, page 18, dwelling 110.

[52] Griffith, *Early Estates*, 12.

[53] T.K. Cartmell, *Shenandoah Valley Pioneers and Their Descendants, A History of Frederick County, Virginia, From its Formation in 1738 to 1908* (Winchester: The Eddy Press Corp., 1909), 449.

[54] Confederate Papers Relating to Citizens or Business Firms, 1861–1865, Citizen Richard E. Byrd: image, Fold3.com, (http://www.fold3.com/image/85491448: accessed Nov. 17, 2015); image from

NARA microfilm publication M346.

[55] Union Provost Marshals' File of Paper Relating to Individual Civilians, 1861–1867, Richard E. Byrd: image, Fold3.com, (http://www.fold3.com/image/280261645: accessed Nov. 17, 2015); image from NARA microfilm publication M345.

[56] Obituary, Wednesday, Jan. 3, 1872, Death of Col. R. E. Byrd, *Winchester Times*, page 2, col. 1, page 3, col. 2, Library of Virginia: The Virginia Newspaper Project Microfilm Collection, 2007, Accessed at Stewart Bell Archive, Handley Library, Winchester, Virginia; Find A Grave Index, 1600s-Current, database, *Ancestry.com*, http://www.ancestry.com: accessed Nov. 27, 2015, entry for Richard Evelyn Byrd, Clarke County, Virginia.

[57] Case Files of Applications from Former Confederates for Presidential Pardons (Amnesty Papers) 1865–1867, Richard E. Byrd: image, Fold3.com, (http://www.fold3.com/image/23926460: accessed Nov. 17, 2015); image from NARA microfilm publication M1003.

[58] Kalbian and Boyer, *Final Report, Historic Context Clarke County*, 15.

[59] Ibid, 15.

[60] Hiatt: *Tax Lists*, 2: 154.

[61] John H. Worsham, *One of Jackson's Foot Cavalry, His Experience and What He Saw During the War 1861–1865, Including a History of F Company, 21st Regiment Virginia Infantry*, (New York: Neale Publishing, 1912), 267.

[62] Kalbian and Boyer, *Final Report, Historic Context Clarke County*, 20.

[63] Hiatt: *Tax Lists*, 2: 177, 199.

[64] Mary Morris, Clarke County Historical Association Interview, March 24, 2016: Samuel J. C. Moore married Ellen Kownlsar, daughter of Dr. Randolph Kownslar from his first wife—possibly Mary McCleary.

[65] Clarke County, Virginia Deed Book I: 204-205. (dtd Dec. 14, 1869, rec Jan. 6, 1870).

[66] 1870 U.S. Census, *Ancestry.com*, (http://www.ancestry.com: accessed March 12, 2016), database entry for Thomas Laws, Clarke County, Virginia, page 29, dwelling 178.

[67] Meyers and Brown, *Annals of Clarke*, 4: 81.

[68] J.G. Randall and David Donald, *The Civil War and Reconstruction* (Boston: D.C. Heath and Company, 1961), 549.

[69] Hiatt: *Tax Lists*, 2: 220.

[70] Meyers and Brown, *Annals of Clarke County Virginia*, 4: 81.

[71] Clarke County, Virginia, Deed Book M: 220. (dtd July 22, 1874, rec March 24, 1876).

[72] Meyers and Brown, *Annals of Clarke County Virginia*, 4: 81.

[73] Clarke County, Virginia, Deed Book K: 104–110. (dtd Sep. 30, 1870, rec Dec. 8, 1871).

[74] Randall and Donald, *The Civil War and Reconstruction*, 550.

[75] Robert Sutton and John Latschar, eds., *The Reconstruction Era, Official National Park Service Handbook*, (Fort Washington, Pennsylvania: Eastern National, 2016) 63.

[76] Clarke County, Virginia, Will Book F: 591. (Edward D. Massey Sale Bill dtd March 21, 1876, rec May 22, 1876).

[77] Clarke County, Virginia, Will Book 1A: 358. (William D. McGuire Sale Bill dtd May 2, 1878, rec June 15, 1878).

[78] Clarke County, Virginia, Marriage Register 1, 1865–1879: 242. Thomas Laws and Bettie Jenkins.

[79] Clarke County, Virginia, Chancery Book E: 217.

[80] Clarke County, Virginia, Deed Book Q: 227–228. (dtd Jan. 30, 1881, rec Jan. 31, 1882).

[81] Local items, Thursday, June 15, 1882, Briefs, *The Clarke Courier*, page 3, col. 1, Library of Virginia, Microfilm Collection, Accessed at Stewart Bell Archive, Handley Library, Winchester, Virginia.

[82] 1880 U.S. Census, database and images, *Ancestry.com* (http://www.ancestry.com: accessed Nov. 2, 2015), entry for Thomas Laws, Clarke County, Virginia. page 18, dwelling 110.

[83] Clarke County, Virginia, Marriage Register 2, 1879–1890: 38. Charles Laws and Mary McCard.

[84] Laws marker, plot W-E-28; personal observation, 2017.

[85] Clarke County, Virginia, Will Book G: 507. (Sale Bill dtd Dec. 24, 1886, rec Jan. 4, 1887).

[86] Compiled by Survivors Association Secretary, *History of the Twenty Third Pennsylvania Volunteer Infantry, Birney's Zouaves*, (Philadelphia: Survivors' Association Twenty-third Regiment, 1903–1904), 169.
Minutes of United Confederate Veterans, J.E.B. Stuart Camp No. 24, Berryville, dated Nov. 26, 1904, denotes a presentation by A[mmishaddai] Moore Jr. on an old Negro man Thomas Laws, former Clarke County slave, who delivered information from Rebecca Wright, a Quakeress in the town of Winchester, to Gen. Sheridan. (Minutes of the Nov. 26, 1904, meeting from the original record of the J.E.B. Stuart Camp, Confederate Veterans of Clarke County. The record book, catalog #1939.00107.001, [restricted by condition] is in the archives of the Clarke County Historical Association, 32 E. Main St., Berryville, Virginia) .

[87] Association Secretary, *History of the Twenty Third Pennsylvania*, 169.

[88] Laws marker, plot W-E-28; personal observation, 2017.

[89] Clarke County, Virginia, Deed Book T: 443. (dtd April 30, 1883, rec Feb. 25, 1885).

[90] 1900 U.S. Census, database and images, *Ancestry.com* (http://www.ancestry.com: accessed March 12, 2016), entry for Charles Laws, Battletown, Clarke County, Virginia. sheet 5A, dwelling 97.

[91] 1910 U.S. Census, database and images, *Ancestry.com*

(http://www.ancestry.com: accessed March 12, 2016), entry for Charles Laws, Berryville, Clarke County, Virginia. Sheet 2A, dwelling 35.

[92] 1920 U.S. Census, database and images, *Ancestry.com* (http://www.ancestry.com: accessed March 12, 2016), entry for Charles Laws, Battletown, Clarke County, Virginia. sheet 8B, dwelling 144.

[93] Clarke County, Virginia, Death Records, 1912–2014, database and images, *Ancestry.com* (http://www.ancestry.com: accessed March 12, 2016), entry for Charles Laws, Battletown, Clarke County, Virginia. Certificate 20140.

[94] 1920 U.S. Census, database and images, *Ancestry.com* (http://www.ancestry.com: accessed April 6, 2016), entry for Sadie Laws, Chicago, Cook County, Illinois. sheet 8B, dwelling 79.

[95] Taylor, *Taylor Sketchbook*, 355. Rebecca Wright's postscript.

34

Winchester's World War Memorial Project

Gene Schultz

In 2015, Don Karolyi, a Winchester physician, appeared in the Winchester-Frederick County Historical Society offices with two small bronze markers that he had found on Handley Boulevard near his home. He wanted to know about the markers and the two men whose names were on them: Russell Brill and Clifton A. Nelson. His enquiry started a project that led back to events that took place on June 28, 1914, when a Serbian nationalist murdered the Archduke of Austria-Hungary and his wife in the streets of Sarajevo. According to William Manchester, the war that was initiated by the assassinations "was, quite simply, the worst thing that had ever happened."[1]

After more than four years of combat, an armistice went into effect on the 11th hour of the 11th day of the 11th month of 1918. The Treaty of Versailles was signed on June 28, 1919, and the "war to end all wars" was officially over. Approximately 53,000 Americans had died in combat and another 63,000 had died from disease or other causes by the time most of the American Expeditionary Force (AEF) returned to the United States in the spring of 1919.[2]

Remembering the Veterans

While the AEF was still in Europe, the group that would become the American Legion held its first meeting in Paris. The group developed a plan that called for recently returned veterans to form local and state organizations that would send delegates to a national convention late in 1919.

The Robert Y. Conrad Post 21 of the American Legion was formed in Winchester on August 22, 1919, and named in honor of the commander of Company I, 116th Infantry who had been killed in action during the Meuse-Argonne offensive. The post's first commander, Robert T. Barton, earned his law degree from the University of Virginia and served as a captain in the 313th Field Artillery Regiment in the 80th Division. He saw action in both the St. Mihiel and Meuse-Argonne offensives.[3]   Captain Barton resigned his position as post commander to become the American Legion's Virginia state commander for the period 1920–21.

Following Capt. Barton's departure, William A. "Sandy" Baker became the Commander of Post 21. Baker spent 21 months in the Army serving with the 1st Pioneer Infantry and saw action at the Marne and the Meuse-Argonne. He also served in Germany during the occupation of the Rhineland following the Armistice and returned to Virginia in April 1919.[4]

The American Legion made no distinctions in membership with regard to race or military rank; however, segregation was a fact in America during the 1920s. African American veterans formed the Charles H. Willis Post 87 of the American Legion in Winchester in 1919. The post was named for Private Charles H. Willis of the 506th Engineers who had died in France from tuberculosis on September 14, 1918.[5] Post 87 closed in October 1923.[6]

By the time the first state convention of the American Legion, Department of Virginia, was held in Roanoke on October 6, 1919, ninety-one posts had been organized.[7] Two of these posts were in Winchester.

The delegates to the national convention approved the constitution of the American Legion at the first national conference. The preamble of the constitution charged the members, in part, "to uphold and defend the Constitution of the United States of America; to preserve the memories and incidents of our associations in the great wars; and to inculcate a sense of individual obligation to the community, state and nation.[8]

In addition to the American Legion wanting to preserve the memories of the Great War, the Commonwealth of Virginia wanted to record as much of the state's involvement in the war as possible. The Virginia War History Commission formed in 1919 and made requests for communities across the state to file reports using a standard format for consistency. The commission sought information on such topics as prewar conditions in the locality, church involvement, school and college involvement, local draft board activities, and casualties. Casualties were to be distinguished between the white and African American populations.

The Virginia War History Commission provided questionnaires to returning soldiers, sailors, marines, and nurses. Each person was asked for information regarding his or her race, religion, education, occupation, military training, rank, service, wounds, and discharge. The questionnaires also asked the individuals how the war experiences had changed their lives.

In Winchester, C. Vernon Eddy, director of the Handley Library, made requests for pictures and information in March 1919 on behalf of the Chamber of Commerce.[9] He later served as the editor of the Virginia War Commission report, *Winchester and Frederick County in War Time*. Frank H. Krebs wrote the first draft of the report between 1919–23 and named 20 white soldiers, four African American soldiers, and one sailor from Winchester and Frederick County who were known to have died during the war. The report cited the Virginia Adjutant General's office as the source of the information but stated that the list "is probably incomplete, since there are at least several persons who died or were killed in action whose names do not appear."[10] The report did not name the missing individuals.

Winchester and Frederick County 1919–24

Much of the United States suffered from an economic downturn following the war. After a brief slowdown immediately after the war, Winchester and Frederick County made tremendous economic progress in the early 1920s. The woolen industry that had remained strong during the war shifted to peacetime production. The commercial apple industry expanded the acreage under cultivation and increased the capacity for processing the crop.

Developers marketed new housing subdivisions in the Virginia Avenue—Smithfield Avenue area on the north side of town as well as along Senseny Road to the east of the city. The Winchester Country Club opened along Senseny Road in 1923.

The Commercial and Savings Bank opened a new building at the corner of East Piccadilly Street and North Loudoun Street. One block east, the George Washington Hotel opened in the summer of 1924. The five-story hotel with its grand lobby and elegant dining room was located between the B&O Railroad passenger station and the downtown business and banking district.

Building of John Handley High School captured both the sense of increasing prosperity and the sense of optimism within Winchester.

Nothing in the region matched the potential impact of the school built on a hill with an investment of $800,000. The first full school year for John Handley High School was 1923–24.

Memorials 1923–24

The fifth anniversary of most of the American combat engagements during the World War occurred in 1923. Veterans' organizations, including the American Legion, planned for memorials to be built and remembrances to be held such as the one for Captain Conrad in October 1923.[12]

The American Legion Weekly magazine published a series of articles in the March 16, April 27, and June 22, 1923, editions on how a community should select a war memorial. Written by combat veteran and nationally recognized sculptor Robert Aitken, the articles warned against buying monuments from jobbers representing granite and metal manufacturers. The articles commented negatively on Civil War memorials that had been placed in communities that showed soldiers standing at parade rest. Aitken stated that the use of "the same figure, same overcoat, same rifle, same position" resulted in "dead, monotonous, meaningless repetition of design" due to the "poor taste on the part of the committee of selection."[13]

Winchester's Civil War memorial, a bronze statue of soldier at rest, was placed on the courthouse grounds in November 1916, represented the Confederate soldiers of Winchester and Frederick County. It was within the range of what Aitkens considered an "artistic atrocity" that should not be repeated when honoring those who had fought in the war.[14]

Accompanying the article in the April 25, 1923, edition was an artist's rendering of an aerial view of the memorial park being planned by the American Legion in Flushing, New York. The 15-acre site included ball fields, a running track, a large flagpole, and trees planted in memory of fallen soldiers with a bronze plaque displaying their names.[15]

The picture of the New York facility bore a resemblance to the Handley High School campus that was still under construction. The landscape plan for Handley High School's 40-acre campus had been developed by John Charles Olmsted of the nationally recognized Olmsted Brothers firm of Brookline, Massachusetts.[16]

The June 22, 1923, *American Legion Weekly* carried the final installment of the Aitken articles. Among the recommendations to be considered as a suitable World War memorial, Aitken proposed a park with symmetry of form laid out for playground and park purposes so improved and maintained.[17]

William A. and Ellen "Nellie" Baker received the *American Legion Weekly* and had access to the Aitken articles. The Bakers lived four blocks from the Handley campus that met the criteria established by Aitken for a suitable World War memorial.

Nellie Baker, president of the Post 21 Auxiliary, was selected to represent the Virginia American Legion Auxiliary at the National American Legion conference in San Francisco in October 1923. Conference presenters encouraged local posts to work with schools in their communities and to support beautification projects.[18]

Baker returned to Winchester in November 1923 and went to work. *The Winchester Evening Star* carried an article on April 12, 1924, stating that five organizations in the city had agreed to support a project to create Memorial Avenue leading up to the new Handley High School. West Gerrard Street between Braddock Street and the school would be the renamed Memorial Avenue and a red oak tree would be planted along the avenue for each of the men from the community who had fallen during the war or since its conclusion. The plan also called for a bronze plate bearing the name of the memorialized individual to be attached to the street curb in front of his tree.[19]

Those involved in the decision to create Winchester's war memorial included Nellie Baker, representing the American Legion Auxiliary; William A. Baker, representing the American Legion as past post commander; City Manager L. R. Dettra, representing the city of Winchester; C. Vernon Eddy and John Steck, representing the recently formed Winchester Parks Commission; and Louisa Green, accompanied by her husband Melvin, representing the Civic League.[20]

The writer for the *Winchester Evening Star* omitted several well-known facts about the committee members. In 1924, William A. Baker served as a member of the City Council; C. Vernon Eddy served as the secretary for the Handley Board of Trustees, the individuals responsible for the construction of Handley High School; and John Steck served as the president of the School Board. It was also known that the Parks Commission and the Civic League both encouraged the planting of trees within the community. The writer could have stated that the plan for the Memorial Avenue had endorsements from the leadership of American Legion and the American Legion Auxiliary, officers of the Handley Board of Trustees and the School Board, a member of City Council and the city manager, and two organizations promoting the planting of trees within the city.

The committee members saw that Memorial Avenue—a grand, oak-lined street leading up to the community's largest building— was the community's statement of its investment in the future through the education of its children. It could also become a living memorial to those who had defended the concepts of liberty and democracy. Incorporated as part of a landscape plan designed by a nationally recognized firm with an assurance of maintenance well into the future, the trees and the memorial markers would add quiet dignity to an already magnificent design.

The optimism and economic prosperity seen in Winchester and Frederick County were visible throughout the Shenandoah Valley in the spring of 1924. The federal highway system expanded and the improved road system made tourism marketable. The federal and state governments considered the creation of a new national park in the Blue Ridge Mountains that would be named Shenandoah. Community leadership throughout the region considered ways to capitalize on tourism and to market the products made in the Valley.

Three days after the Memorial Avenue announcement, the April 15, 1924, Winchester Evening Star carried a front-page article on a proposed economic development project to promote the Shenandoah Valley and the apple industry. The project was to be known as the Shenandoah Apple Blossom Festival and the proposal called for the festival to be held in Winchester on the first weekend in May.

The three weeks between the announcement of the event and the festival were very busy for the organizing committee. The activities included a visit by festival representatives to the White House to extend an invitation personally to President Calvin Coolidge.

Staff writers for the *Winchester Evening Star* displayed the excitement and the national recognition of the first Apple Blossom Festival in their reporting. The front page of the paper on Monday, May 5, 1924, carried a picture of the Winchester delegation at the White House, a series of reports on the festival that had been held on Saturday, an article in which the local Ku Klux Klan blamed out of town Klan members for the burning of a cross at city hall during the festival, and an article stating that Secretary of War John Weeks, representing the President of the United States at the Apple Blossom Festival, had planted the first war memorial tree on the Handley campus.[21]

The article stated the following:

> The first of the trees to be planted under the auspices of the ladies auxiliary of the American Legion in memory of deceased Winchester and Frederick County service men of the world war was planted by Secretary of War John W. Weeks who was the guest of Dr. and Mrs. Robert M. Glass during the Apple Blossom festival.
>
> The invitation to plant the first memorial tree was extended to Mr. Weeks shortly after his arrival here and he readily accepted the invitation. He expressed gratification that the local legion post auxiliary had taken up the matter of planting trees in memory of the Winchester and Frederick County men who had given their lives during the war.
>
> Mr. Weeks and his party were accompanied to the Handley school grounds where the trees were to be planted and after a hole had been dug the secretary planted the tree, tramped the earth around it and made a brief speech.
>
> Chairman John W. Steck of the city school board and

other members of the board together with R. Gray Williams, president of the Handley Board of Trustees, and many others were present at the simple ceremony.

The following day, through a letter to the editor of the *Winchester Evening Star*, Ellen Baker made it very clear that the American Legion Auxiliary had not invited the Secretary of War to plant the first memorial tree, and in fact, had not even been notified of the event. She stated that the executive committee of the American Legion Auxiliary had recommended that the dedication of the trees would be held on June 6, 1924 as part of the Confederate Memorial Day celebration and that proper notifications would be made at that time.[22]

The *Winchester Evening Star* ran a clarification on May 7 in which it stated,

> The tree planted here last Saturday by Secretary of War Weeks is on the Handley School grounds it was learned today and is not on what is to be officially designated as "Memorial Avenue."

> The tree which is a white birch about 10 feet high and at present is without any leaves is almost directly opposite the garage of W. G. Hardy's residence and it is about 50 feet back from the sidewalk on the south side of Gerrard Street.

> The tree however is in the immediate vicinity of Memorial Avenue.[23]

In the same edition of the paper, a letter to the editor from J. M. Steck, president of the School Board, offered an explanation and clarification of the tree planting incident.

Letter to the editor

> In your paper yesterday Mrs. W. A. Baker, as president of the American Legion Auxiliary, wrote an article based upon the erroneous impression that Secretary of War Weeks had planted a tree on the Handley grounds in memory of our soldiers who fell in the great war.

Mrs. Baker's erroneous impression was due to an article printed in your paper that made the mistake of inferring that Secretary of War Weeks had planted a tree as a memorial to our dead soldiers, when in fact the tree planted by Secretary of War Weeks had nothing whatever to do with the trees the American Legion has planted and expects to dedicate to the memory of their fallen comrades.

Just before the parade the idea occurred to me that the School Board and Handley Board were planting trees and that it would be interesting to commemorate the coming of the Secretary of War in blossom time by having him plant one of these trees.

I saw the Secretary's host, Dr. Robert Glass, and Mr. R. Gray Williams who was with the Secretary, as he had been designated to introduce him, and went in Dr. Glass's car to the grounds where the secretary planted a tree without any particular ceremony. There was not one word said about the memorial to soldiers and there was no thought of the tree having any connection with a memorial to the soldiers.

Secretary of War Weeks came here as the representative of President Coolidge upon an occasion that signified the felicitations of this community over its importance as an apple center. His visit had nothing to do with war or war memorials.

J. M. Steck
President, School Board

The tree planting report and subsequent newspaper articles show that trees were being planted on the Handley campus in early May 1924 and that trees were already being planted on Memorial Avenue approximately three weeks after the plan had been announced. The American Legion Auxiliary Executive Committee planned to have the trees planted and dedicated in less than two months.

The *Winchester Evening Star* on May 20, 1924, carried an article that stated the American Legion Auxiliary at its regular meeting had decided not to dedicate the trees on June 6, Confederate Memorial Day, but rather to wait until November 11, Armistice Day, for the dedication even though the crowd might be smaller. The American Legion Auxiliary also decided at that meeting to provide the bronze plaques with the names of the fallen that would be placed in the curb near each memorial tree.[24] The organization released no listing of the names of the soldiers to be memorialized or the number of trees to be planted at that time.

On August 1, 1924, the *Winchester Evening Star* carried an article with the title "Honor Roll of Our Dead Boys Is Here Given." The Memorial Committee of the American Legion Auxiliary stated that their list was the first list of casualties from the area that could be discovered, that it had been very difficult to obtain the information, and that the list may be incomplete. The committee named forty-one men who had "made the supreme sacrifice in the service or have died since the Armistice."

The committee asked the community for any names, both male and female, that might have been missed. The committee also requested the community's help to contact the families of the men named in order to have them attend the Armistice Day dedication.

The Memorial Committee then added a statement about the trees. "These red oaks that shall eventually shade our Memorial Avenue splendidly typify those whose names they bear. The small acorn from which they sprung, being the service from the soldiers point of view; the eventual great red oak being symbolic of the soldier's service from a community point of view."[25]

The pamphlet *Winchester and Frederick County in War Time*, as edited by C. Vernon Eddy, named 25 men on the Gold Star List. The manuscript for the document stated that Captain Conrad and thirty-three other men from the vicinity had died overseas or in the camps during the war.[26] The thirty-three additional men were not identified.

Nellie Baker provided a "corrected" list of soldiers for publication in the *Winchester Evening Star* on September 3, 1924. The list included 45 names of men who had died during the war or in the nearly 6 years since the Armistice. Mrs. Baker requested that those with knowledge of any additional names or corrections in names contact her with appropriate documentation by early October to ensure a bronze plaque could be acquired before the November 11 dedication.[27]

By late October the list had grown to 49 names. The last additions included Ramey Kerns who died October 7, 1924, and Alexander J. Nielson, "an Esquimo." The spelling of Edward V. Willey was changed to Edward V. Willie.

Armistice Day 1924

Winchester's 1924 Armistice Day celebration became a two-day event orchestrated by the American Legion and directed by Nellie Baker. It centered on the dedication of the Memorial Avenue trees and plaques.

The activities started on Monday, November 10, with an evening reception and dance at the Baker home on South Washington Street. Guests included the national president of the American Legion Auxiliary, the state commander of the American Legion, the chairman of the National Legislative Committee of the American Legion and members of the executive committees of neighboring posts and post auxiliaries.[28]

The Armistice Day program for Tuesday, November 11, 1924, had a full schedule beginning at 9:00 a.m., when members of the Post 21 Auxiliary were asked to meet at City Hall to prepare for the parade. The plan called for the parade to leave City Hall in time to reach the Handley campus by 10:45 am. The damp, cold weather improved to partly sunny conditions by 11:00 a.m., the hour that the Armistice had become effective in France on November 11, 1918, and the scheduled time for the dedication services to begin.

Reverend Robert Nelson, rector of Christ Episcopal Church and chaplain of Post 21 announced the remembrance hour on the Handley campus as church bells and fire bells rang across the city. Buglers played "Taps," which was followed by a moment of silent prayer. "America" was then played by the Citizens Band.

Major Robert T. Barton served as master of ceremonies for the dedication of exercises. He welcomed the guests to Winchester and greeted the families of the men being memorialized. He then introduced the national president of the American Legion Auxiliary and the Virginia Department commander of the American Legion.

Phillip Williams, a veteran of the Army Air Corps, gave the dedication address that included a poem written by a member of the Civic League for the occasion. The Citizens Band then played the national anthem before the ceremony ended with a benediction given by Reverend Nelson.

The Bakers provided a buffet luncheon for the department officers and executive committee of the American Legion and American Legion Auxiliary before returning to the Handley Stadium for a football game between Post 21 and the visiting American Legion team from Front Royal. The home team won 21–0.

The football game was followed by an open house and reception at the American Legion Home on North Loudoun Street between 5:00 p.m. and 6:00 p.m. Dinner for American Legion and Auxiliary officers was served prior to a dance at the Baker home to conclude the day's activities.[29]

The 1924 plan called for a gradual expansion of the Memorial Avenue project to include the placement of a memorial plaque along the avenue for the local veterans as they died in the future.

No additional plaques were ever installed as the country went into the Great Depression in 1929 and the world entered a second world war in 1939.

Over time the memorial oak trees died and elements dislodged the bronze markers from the curbing. Individuals recovered displaced markers and kept them as souvenirs. City employees doing street repairs recovered five of the markers and gave them to Handley High School. Most of the markers, however, were lost.

By the time Memorial Avenue had become Handley Boulevard, most of the citizens of Winchester and Frederick County had forgotten about the memorial trees, the markers, and the men who had died as a result of their service in the First World War.

Dr. Karolyi's recovery of the two damaged markers and his

enquiry started the Winchester-Frederick County Historical Society's project that eventually involved numerous groups in Winchester and Frederick County as well as researchers in Virginia, West Virginia, Delaware, Pennsylvania, and Indiana. By the end of 2017, the Society had located 15 of the original markers and acquired a picture of another.

Most of the communities in the region created World War memorials during the 1920s but Winchester's Memorial Avenue project was unique. It had no statues of soldiers or bronze tablets with the names of all who had served. It honored the fallen equally with no distinctions made for rank, race, or national origin. It was designed to be a living memorial that could be expanded, replaced, and refurbished over time.

Nearly a century later, the community is once again remembering those who served in the World War.

Those Honored

The writings of C. Vernon Eddy, Frank H. Krebs, and Ellen Baker all indicate that no comprehensive list of the local men and women who died during the war ever existed. Variations in the spelling of names and ties to multiple localities made it almost impossible to identify all.

Although described throughout the 1924 Memorial Avenue project as being youth from Winchester and Frederick County, several of the men who received memorial plaques were not from the community. Among the 49 who received plaques are men who were also memorialized in five additional Virginia counties as well as the states of West Virginia, Kentucky, Pennsylvania, and New York. However, each did have a connection to the community.

Two of the men who received memorial plaques were brothers from Winchester. Two of the men were cousins from the Shockeysville area of Frederick County. One man was not an American citizen and one was a draft evader.

Sixteen of the 49 men who received plaques were killed in action or were mortally wounded and died in France. Four of the men were gassed in France and died in the United States during the first six years after the Armistice.

Forty seven of the 49 have been identified and a short biography of each, in alphabetical order, follows. Two of the 49, Carroll Jenkins and Edward V. Willie have not been positively identified.

The first soldier from Frederick County identified as killed in action was **Private Thomas Garrett Adams**. A resident of Gainesboro, he had gone to Martinsburg, West Virginia, to work in the woolen mills at the beginning of the war. He was 32 years old when drafted from Martinsburg on April 2, 1918, and sent to Camp Lee, Virginia, for basic training. He went to France as a private in Company L of the 320th Infantry and was killed by artillery on September 28, 1918. His body was returned to Winchester from Brieulles-sur-Meuse, France, in September 1921 and was reinterred in Mount Hebron Cemetery. Approaching her 100th birthday, his niece, the late Francis Adams Unger, remembered his memorial service in Mount Hebron Cemetery and how the firing of a volley in his honor had scared her when she was 4 years old.[31]

Private Clifton W. Anderson was on C. Vernon Eddy's list of men from the area who died during the war. His draft registration card shows he was born at Gore, Virginia on October 27, 1892 and that he worked as an assistant engineer for the Sinclair Refrigeration Company. The manuscript record of men drafted from Winchester-Frederick County shows he was drafted in June 1917 and sent to Camp Lewis, Washington, for training.[32] Arlington National Cemetery has the grave of Clifton W. Anderson from Washington State who served with the 109th Infantry and died in France on November 16, 1918.[33]

The only member of the United States Navy from Winchester and Frederick County who died during the war was **Seaman Apprentice Samuel Dean Baker** from Cross Junction. He resigned from the Washington, D.C., police force to enlist in December 1917, and was sent to Norfolk Naval Station. He died at the age of 23 from spinal meningitis on March 1, 1918.[34] He was buried in Mount Hebron Cemetery.

Corporal Russell Thomas Beatty served in Company E, 319th Infantry. His draft registration card indicates he was born in

Berryville, Virginia, on November 11, 1894. The son of a music teacher, he lived in Middletown and near Gainesboro before moving to Pricedale, Pennsylvania, where he worked as a tripper for Pittsburgh Steel. At the time of his death, Corporal Beatty's parents lived in Bluemont, Virginia.[35] He was wounded on September 26 and died on October 3, 1918.[36] Corporal Beatty was buried in Arlington National Cemetery.

William Avenel Beverley died from heart failure at the Winchester home of his parents on November 6, 1920. He served in the Ordnance Department of the Army during the war and spent approximately 1 year in France before returning home in April 1919. He completed a Virginia War History Commission questionnaire on November 20, 1919, in Youngstown, Ohio, in which he stated that he had seen a great deal of fighting while acting as a conveyer of ammunition and guns.[37] He returned to Winchester in 1920 to work in the apple industry. He was the brother-in-law of Harry F. Byrd and was buried in Mount Hebron Cemetery.[38]

Sergeant Milford Bolner served with Company I, 116th Infantry. Born near Zepp in Shenandoah County, he worked at the Snapp Foundry in Winchester before moving to Chester, Pennsylvania. He returned to Virginia to accompany Company I to the Mexican border and, after the Company's return, he remained in Virginia until the unit was called into federal service. Sergeant Bolner's family moved to Ashland, Kentucky about 1916.[39] Sergeant Bolner was killed in action on October 15, 1918, during the attack on Grande Montagne. He was buried in Arlington National Cemetery.

Private Thomas Vernon Bowers was a painter from Rest, Virginia. He was drafted and sent to Camp Lee in June 1918, where he died from pneumonia on October 5, 1918. He was buried at Rest United Methodist Church.[40]

Private Russell Brill from Maurertown, Virginia, died from disease while in training with Company I, 116th Infantry at Camp McClellan, Alabama, on February 18, 1918. He was buried beside his mother at Union Forge Cemetery near Edinburg, Virginia.

William Marshall Cadwallader from Vaucluse, Virginia was a student at Roanoke College where he had enlisted as a member of the Student's Army Training Corps. A 1918 graduate of Middletown High School, he died October 31, 1918, having returned to Roanoke a week earlier following the funeral of his father. Both men died from pneumonia following influenza and both were buried at Green Hill Cemetery in Stephens City.[41]

Captain Lucien Carr III was a native of Winchester and lived in the city before moving to Washington. D.C. Assigned to the Army Transport Service, 806th Stevedore Battalion, he was in charge of the electrical work at the port of St. Nazaire, France. He developed pneumonia after being exposed to bad weather while working at the port and died on November 20, 1918. Captain Carr was buried at Oise-Aisne American Cemetery in France and has a marker at the family plot in Mount Hebron Cemetery.[42]

Captain Robert Young Conrad was the commanding officer of Company I, 116th Infantry. He took the unit to the Mexican border in 1916 and led the unit through its training at Camp McClellan near Anniston, Alabama, before being deployed to France. He was mortally wounded in the company of several enlisted men during the attack on Ormond Farm on October 8, 1918, during the Meuse-Argonne offensive. He was posthumously awarded the Distinguished Service Cross and was buried in the Meuse-Argonne American cemetery in Romagne-sous-Montfaucon, France.

The announcement of Captain Conrad's death appeared in the November 4, 1918, edition of the *Winchester Evening Star*. The writer stated that Captain Conrad was the first Winchester soldier killed in battle. The statement was incorrect, but, due to the delays in reporting casualties from France, the notification appears to have been the first to arrive in Winchester.

The Virginia Adjutant General's report of casualties had been published by the time Frank Krebs and C. Vernon Eddy drafted Winchester and Frederick County in War Time. Using the dates provided by the Adjutant General's report, Mr. Krebs noted that Captain Conrad was the first officer from the area killed in combat and Mr. Eddy made no distinction as to the first killed in the report.[43]

In his final book, *Some Worthy Lives*, local historian Garland Quarles told the story of Captain Conrad by recalling the *Winchester Evening Star* article of November 4, 1918. He wrote of the well-known, 34 year-old attorney that the "death of Captain Conrad came as a shock to the people of Winchester, not only because of his deserved popularity, but because it was the first death of a Winchester citizen in the war."[44]

Private Isaac Byrd Dix from White Hall, Virginia, died of pneumonia following influenza at Camp Humphrey, Virginia, on October 1, 1918. He was in training with Company F of the 5th Engineers. He was buried with his family at the Old Stone Church at Green Spring.[45]

Private Silas Edward Fauver was a self-employed machinist from Mount Williams, Virginia. He was drafted from Frederick County on April 2, 1918 and assigned to Company C, 315th Machine Gun Battalion, 80th Division. He died as a result of disease and fever on June 28, 1918, in the Nord-Pas de Calais region, France. Following the war his body was reinterred in Arlington National Cemetery.[46]

Private Thurman Fletcher was a farmer from Whitacre who died of disease at Camp Lee, Virginia, on August 11, 1918. He was buried at Ebenezer Christian Church near Gore, Virginia.

Lieutenant Benjamin Pierson Ford was a member of Company L, 352nd Infantry serving with the 80th Division. A native of East Orange, New Jersey, he came to Winchester before the war to assist his grandfather, Professor George Shepard, manage several orchards in the area. He was interested in the work of the government entomologists who had established a headquarters here and frequently sang in the choir at Christ Episcopal Church. Drafted from Winchester in October 1917 and sent to Camp Lee, he was quickly promoted to Sergeant. Arriving in France he was sent to officer training school and was subsequently promoted to Second Lieutenant.[47] He was killed by an enemy hand grenade on October 28, 1918, in the Alsace region of France.[48] Lieutenant Ford's body was returned from France and reinterred in Morristown, New Jersey, on January 15, 1921.[49]

Lohr Foreman died in a traffic accident in Washington, D.C., on October 15, 1919, when the streetcar he was riding collided with an Army truck near Walter Reed Hospital. A native of Hayfield, Virginia, he had returned to the United States from France in August 1919. He was buried at Ebenezer Church near Gore, Virginia.[50]

Private John Henry Golliday lived at Vaucluse, Virginia. He served in Company I, 317th Infantry, 80th Division. He contracted tuberculosis while in the Army and his death certificate states he died of tuberculosis of the lung following influenza on January 22, 1920, at his parents' home.[51] He was buried at Salem Church of the Brethren near Stephens City.

Private Charles Emmett Graber died in the United States Public
Health Service Hospital in Washington, D. C., on May 5, 1920. A
native of Winchester, he had moved to New Haven, Connecticut,
prior to the war and had worked as an architectural drafter. He
returned from France after the Armistice and was admitted to the
United States Public Health Service Hospital in New Haven, a
center for the treatment of tuberculosis. Following services at
Christ Episcopal Church, he was buried in Mount Hebron
Cemetery.[52]

Private George Barrow Grim died on a transport ship en route to
France on October 9, 1918. The *Winchester Evening Star* reported
that it was presumed he had been buried at sea. His cousin,
Mildred Grim Brumback, stated that his body had been returned
from France in 1924 and that he had been buried beside his father
at Ridings Chapel United Methodist Church in Frederick County.[53]

Sergeant James Frank Hinton was from Clearbrook, Virginia, and served with Company I, 116th Infantry during the Mexican border conflict and in France.[54] He was killed in action on October 15, 1918, during the assault on Grande Montagne and was buried in Mount Hebron Cemetery.

Private Carl M. Jenkins was a member of the Presbyterian Church at Vaucluse. He joined the Army on October 1, 1917, and was deployed to France with Company H of the 19th Engineers. Following an extended illness, he died at U.S. Army Hospital Number 4 near Paris on July 30, 1918. He had a church funeral with full military honors prior to his burial in a small military cemetery near Paris.[55] His body was returned to the United States and was reinterred at Mount Carmel Cemetery in Middletown.

Private Solomon Johnson, an African-American draftee, was identified as the first soldier from Winchester to be killed in action. He was drafted from Winchester and was assigned to New York National Guard's 15th Infantry that was based in Harlem. The unit later became part of the 369th Infantry. Known as the Harlem Hellfighters, the unit was first assigned to the American 93rd Division before being assigned to the French 161st Division. The 369th Infantry fought with French colonial troops from North Africa and Senegal.[56] Private Johnson was listed as missing in action and later as killed in action on October 2, 1918. His name is on the tablet for those missing in action at the Meuse-Argonne American Cemetery Romagne-sous-Montfaucon, France.[57]

Private Homer Caleb Kerns was a member of the 5th Engineers and died of disease in France on December 2, 1918. His body was reinterred at Wesley Chapel near Cross Junction.[58]

Private Ramey Beldon Kerns was a private in Company I, 116th Infantry. The newspaper article reporting his death stated he had been the first to reach Captain Robert Conrad after the officer had been mortally wounded and that Private Kerns was gassed during a subsequent engagement in October 1918. He never fully recovered.[59] He died at the Nanticoke State Hospital in Nanticoke, Pennsylvania, on October 7, 1924, and was buried at Mount Olive United Methodist Church near Hayfield, Virginia.

Private Alva Lichliter served in Company I, 38th Infantry and was killed in action October 5, 1918, during part of the Meuse-Argonne offensive. He was born in Winchester and raised near Gore, Virginia. He was drafted from Ashland, Kentucky, where he worked with his brothers as a dry cleaner. At the time his brother's obituary was published on January 4, 1919, Private Lichliter was listed as a survivor, which indicates the family had not been notified of his death three months earlier.[60] Private Lichliter was buried at the Meuse-Argonne American Cemetery in Romagne-sous-Montfaucon, France.

Private First Class William Locke served with Company I, 2nd Virginia Infantry Regiment during the Mexican border campaign and rejoined Company I during the summer of 1917. He contracted tuberculosis while in training at Camp McClellan near Anniston,

Alabama, and was sent to Camp Bayard in New Mexico for treatment. He was released from the hospital and discharged from the Army on April 14, 1919. He returned to Winchester and worked for the Virginia Woolen Company until hospitalized at the United State Public Health Service hospital at Fort McHenry near Baltimore where he died of tuberculosis on March 6, 1921.[61] Private Locke was buried in Mount Hebron Cemetery.

Private Floyd Lucas served with Company I, 116th Infantry and was killed during the same attack on Grande Montagne as Sergeant Bolner and Sergeant Hinton. A native of Stanley, Virginia, his body was returned home where he was buried in an unmarked grave on the family farm in 1919.[62]

Private Oscar Lee Luttrell lived in Morgan County, West Virginia. *The Morgan News* carried an article regarding his death that stated he "had died in a hospital in Martinsburg of typhoid fever on August 9. He had been ill for several weeks. He was attacked with typhoid while in camp and his parents were permitted to remove him to the hospital two weeks before his death. Young Luttrell was the young fellow who attempted, and did for awhile, evade the draft but was apprehended near Martinsburg and sent to an encampment." He was 23 years old and was buried at Shockeysville United Methodist Church cemetery in August 1918.[63]

Private Smith Nathaniel Luttrell from Shockeysville, Virginia, was the cousin of Oscar Lee Luttrell. He died of pneumonia at Camp Upton, New York, on October 11, 1918. He was 23 years old.[64] He was buried at the Shockeysville United Methodist Church.

Corporal James Overton McNeill was an insurance agent from Moorefield, West Virginia, who married Margaret Larrick of Winchester. Assigned to the Quartermaster Corps, 358th Infantry, he deployed from Camp Lee on August 25, 1918, and died of pneumonia in France on October 13.[65] He was buried at the St. Mihiel American Cemetery near Thiaucourt, France.[66]

Private Arthur Nelson was a farmer from Highview, West Virginia. He died from influenza and pneumonia at Camp Holabird near Baltimore, Maryland, on October 10, 1918. His brothers were C. A. Nelson who had a laundry business in Winchester and Harry and Edgar Nelson who were at home. He was buried at Timber Ridge Christian Church.[67]

Private Clifton A. Nelson died from pneumonia at Camp Lee on October 10, 1918. Born in Warren County, his family had a farm near Fawcett's Gap in Frederick County. According to his family, his body could have been sent to the farm where it was buried in a now lost grave. His wife and young son relocated to west Texas where his descendants now live.[68]

Private Alexander Nielson (Axel Julius Nielsen)
One of the last men nominated to receive a memorial plaque was listed as Alexander J. Nielson, an "Esquimo." Nielson arrived in Winchester with a detachment from Camp Lee to harvest apples on September 28, 1918. Several of the soldiers were hospitalized for influenza immediately upon arrival and two soldiers died in the Winchester hospital within days. Both soldiers were from western Pennsylvania. The fourth member of the detachment to die was Alexander Nielson.

Up to 15 of the 99 soldiers assigned to pick apples in Frederick County died from complications from influenza. All of their bodies were sent to their homes except Nielson's as apparently no one knew where to send it. The War Department notified officials in Winchester that he should be buried with the Union soldiers in the National Cemetery after the body had been at the Kurtz Funeral Home for a week.[69]

The death certificate completed in Winchester stated that Alex. J. Nielson, a male Esquimo of unknown age assigned to the 4th Company of the 1st Battalion from Camp Lee had died in the Memorial Hospital on October 10, 1918, as a result of influenza. The certificate showed that information had been taken from the orders found on the body and that it had been determined his nearest friend was Mabel Jacobson of Summit Street in Brooklyn, New York.[70]

The *Winchester Evening Star* reported his funeral on October 18, 1918. The reporter stated that the soldier received no religious service, and that his flag-covered coffin was carried by other soldiers from Camp Lee. The Winchester State Guard fired a volley in his honor.[71] He was buried beside members of the Vermont cavalry in the Winchester National Cemetery under a stone marked only "A. J. Nielsen; USA."

A New York State casualty report noted Axel J. Nielson, born in Denmark on September 27, 1893 was drafted from Houtzdale, Pennsylvania, on August 27, 1918. It stated that Nielson died at an unspecified location from influenza on October 10, 1918. The person to contact in case of death was Mable Jacobson in Brooklyn, New York.[72]

Axel Nielsen's draft registration shows he was a 25 year-old laborer working in Philipsburg, Pennsylvania, in July 1918. A Danish citizen born near Copenhagen, he stated that he was a single Caucasian with no dependents.[73]

Alexander Nielson, the "Esquimo," was actually Axel Julius Nielsen, a Danish citizen who was drafted from western Pennsylvania. Private Nielsen was the only person identified by race or ethnic group in the 1924 newspaper articles.

Private Charles Hubard Cary Oldham completed a Virginia War History Commission questionnaire on July 27, 1921, in Salem, Virginia. He stated that he had been born in Moundsville, West Virginia, on May 18, 1897, and that before the war he had been an architectural drafter for Stuart H. Edmonds in Winchester, Virginia. He had enlisted as a private in the aviation section of the regular Army on August 13, 1917, at Columbus, Ohio and had been assigned to the 97th Aero Squadron. He was deployed to France in November 1917. On March 13, 1918, he entered Base Hospital Number 4 where he remained until May 7, 1918. In response to the question "What were the effects upon yourself of your overseas experience?" he responded, "The contraction of tuberculosis." He was discharged on March 1, 1919.[74]

The *Winchester Evening Star* reported that Private Oldham had been stationed at Rouen where he had been badly gassed and had never completely recovered. He subsequently developed tuberculosis and spent time in Army hospitals in Eudowood, Maryland, and Sawtelle, California, where he died on August 8, 1922.[75] Following his burial in the Bruce family plot in Mount Hebron Cemetery, Christ Episcopal Church, his mother's home church, placed a plaque in his honor in the sanctuary.

Private Charles Henry Orndorff worked on the family farm near Mount Williams prior to being drafted in May 1918. He was killed in action on October 14, 1918, during the Meuse-Argonne offensive. He was buried in the St. Johns Lutheran Cemetery where his gravestone was inscribed with Sir Walter Scott's line "Rest, soldier rest; thy warfare o'er."

Corporal Manly Payne served with Company I, 116th Infantry. He enlisted in 1917 and was deployed to France in June 1918. He was gassed during the unit's attack on Molleville Farm on October 5, 1918, and never recovered from the wounding. Discharged in May 1919, he was hospitalized at Winchester Memorial Hospital in August 1920, and remained there for three months before being transferred to Fort McHenry Hospital near Baltimore for an additional six months. Showing no improvement he was sent home to Clarke County where he died on August 12, 1921. He was buried in Mount Hebron Cemetery.[76]

Sergeant Miles Sanger of Clearbrook, Virginia, served with Company I, 116th Infantry. He was severely wounded in action and died from his wounds on December 4, 1918, in France.[77] He was buried in Arlington National Cemetery.

Corporal Carl Schmidt served in the Brest region of France with the 509th Motor Transport Company. According to *Winchester Evening Star* articles, he was gassed and also hospitalized for influenza while in France. Following the hospitalization he showed signs of tuberculosis. Corporal Schmidt was sent to Army hospitals in North Carolina and Colorado for treatment of tuberculosis. The disease progressed and he was sent home to Winchester where he died at the age of 25 on February 4, 1922, in the home of his German-born parents. Corporal Schmidt was a member of Grace Evangelical Lutheran Church. He was buried in Mount Hebron Cemetery.

Private Raymond Shenk of Reynolds Store served with Company I, 116th Infantry. He was killed in action on October 16, 1918, and was buried at Wesley Chapel near Cross Junction, Virginia.

Lieutenant Louis Edward Snapp was a member of Grace Evangelical Lutheran Church in Winchester and served with Company I of the Second Virginia Regiment during the Mexican border conflict in 1916. By the fall of 1918, he had been promoted to sergeant with the company. He was badly wounded by machine gun fire during the Meuse-Argonne offensive but remained in France where he received a promotion to the rank of second lieutenant and was awarded the French Croix de Guerre for bravery in combat.

Lieutenant Snapp returned to Winchester in June 1919. On July 1, 1919, he was involved as a passenger in an automobile accident on Valley Avenue in which he sustained multiple fractures and internal injuries. He died in the Winchester Memorial Hospital on July 4, 1919, and received full military honors at his burial in Mount Hebron Cemetery.[78]

Corporal Richard Stewart was born in Hampshire County, West Virginia in February 1892. His draft registration, completed in Winchester in June 1917, indicated he was a resident of Winchester but had been employed by the Republic Rubber Company in Youngstown, Ohio. Corporal Stewart served with the 317th Infantry in the 80th Division. He was killed in action November 6, 1918, and was buried in the Meuse-Argonne American Cemetery in Romagne sous Montfaucon, France.[79] A memorial marker was placed in the family plot in the Mount Zion Cemetery near Augusta, West Virginia.

Sergeant Archibald Whittle, a native of Cumberland, Rhode Island, had been employed as a line supervisor with the Western Union Telegraph Company in Richmond, Virginia, prior to war. He married Leuvilla Mae Browning of Frederick County in November 1917.[80] The *Winchester Evening Star* published excerpts from a letter he sent to his wife from the trenches in which he described the inhumanity of the German soldiers toward the British dead left on the battlefield.[81] Sergeant Whittle served in the Signal Corps attached to the 318th Infantry and was killed in action on October 21, 1918. He was buried in the Meuse-Argonne American Cemetery in Romagne-sous-Montfaucon, France.[82]

Private John Conly Wigginton contracted tuberculosis while serving with the Signal Corps squadrons at Vancouver Barracks on the Columbia River. Men assigned to the squadrons worked in logging camps in the Pacific Northwest to harvest lumber for the construction of airplanes. Private Wigginton died from tuberculosis in Winchester at the age of 35 on September 6, 1923. Following a memorial service at the Highland Avenue Mission Church, he was buried in Mount Hebron Cemetery.[83]

The first soldier from Winchester known to have died in service and to receive a World War memorial plaque was **Private Joseph Wright Wigginton** of Company I, 2nd Virginia Infantry. The unit had been assigned to protect vital railroad bridges from possible saboteurs at the beginning of the war and Private Wigginton's unit had been detailed to the Norfolk and Western Railroad bridge at Overall Creek in Page County. Private Wigginton and Corporal Joseph Reid went swimming in the South Fork of the Shenandoah River on June 13, 1917, and both experienced distress while crossing the river. Corporal Reid made it to shore safely but Wigginton drowned. The 18 year-old soldier, the younger brother of J. C. Wigginton, was buried with military honors in Mount Hebron Cemetery.[84]

Private Charles H. Willis worked for the C. L. Robinson Cold Storage Company prior to the war and moved to Pittsburgh just before being drafted in the summer of 1917. He served with the 506th Engineering Corps and died from tuberculosis in France on September 14, 1918. His parents held a memorial service for him at the Orrick Cemetery in Winchester on October 6, 1918.[85] Private Willis' body was returned to Winchester in November

1920, and he was reinterred in the Winchester National Cemetery with military honors provided by members of the Charles H. Willis Post 87 of the American Legion.[86]

Private Walter Gore Wingfield was from Gore, Virginia, and was drafted from Frederick County in May 1918. He served in France with Company F, 6th Ammunition Train and died from pneumonia on April 3, 1919, at the age of 22.[87] His body was returned to Winchester in June 1921, and he was reinterred in the Winchester National Cemetery with full military honors.[88]

Private William Carson Wisecarver lived near Opequon in Frederick County.[89] He died at the age of 23 from pneumonia following influenza at Camp Lee, Virginia, on October 12, 1918. An article following his death in the *Winchester Evening Star* stated that Attorney M. M. Lynch of Winchester had been appointed guardian for Zula Virginia Wisecarver, Private Wisecarver's 18 year-old widow.[90]

Endnotes

[1] William Manchester, *American Caesar, Douglas MacArthur, 1880–1964* (New York: Little, Brown and Company, 1978)

[2] www.va.gov/opa/publications/factsheets/fs_americas_wars.pdf

[3] Virginia War History Commission Military Service Record questionnaire completed by Captain Barton in Winchester on November 19, 1919, State Records Collection, The Library of Virginia, Richmond, Virginia

[4] Virginia War History Commission Military Service Record questionnaire completed by Lt. Baker in Winchester on November 19, 1919, State Records Collection, The Library of Virginia, Richmond, Virginia

[5] *Winchester Evening Star*, October 5, 1918

[6] Information provided by Debra Brookhart, Curator/Archivist, Library Division, American Legion National Office by email on August 3, 2016

[7] Gates R. Richardson, *The American Legion, Department of Virginia, 1919–1969* (Richmond: American Legion, 1982)

[8] Preamble to the Constitution of the American Legion, www.legion.org/mission

[9] *Winchester Evening Star*, March 10, 1919

[10] C. Vernon Eddy, *Winchester and Frederick County in Wartime, A Community History* (Winchester: 1926), Gold Star List

[11] Garland R. Quarles, *The Schools of Winchester, Virginia* (Winchester: Farmers and Merchants National Bank, 1964)

[12] *Winchester Evening Star*, October 8, 1923

[13] *The American Legion Weekly* 5, no.11 (March 16, 1923)

[14] Ibid.

[15] *The American Legion Weekly* 5, no.17 (April 25, 1923)

[16] National Register of Historic Places Registration Form for John Handley High School, completed July 1, 1998, found at www.dhr.virginia.gov

[17] *The American Legion Weekly 5*, no. 25 (June 22, 1923)

[18] *American Legion/American Legion Auxiliary Minutes*, Fifth National Convention, San Francisco, 1923

[19] *Winchester Evening Star*, April 12, 1924

[20] *Winchester Evening Star*, April 12, 1924

[21] *Winchester Evening Star*, May 5, 1924

[22] *Winchester Evening Star*, May 6, 1924

[23] *Winchester Evening Star*, May 7, 1924

[24] *Winchester Evening Star*, May 20, 1924

[25] *Winchester Evening Star*, August 1, 1924

[26] Eddy, *Winchester and Frederick County in War Time*, archives of The Handley Library

[27] *Winchester Evening Star*, September 3, 1924

[28] *Winchester Evening Star*, November 10, 1924

[29] *Winchester Evening Star*, November 12, 1924

[30] Hand written note provided by Francis A. Unger, October 2016

[31] Interview with Francis Unger, October 4, 2016

[32] "Soldiers from Frederick County and Winchester in World War I," World War One Collection, 1115 WFCHS/THL, Stewart Bell Jr. Archives, Handley Regional Library, Winchester, Virginia

[33] www.arlingtoncemetery.mil

[34] *Winchester Evening Star*, March 4, 1918

[35] November 4, 1918

[36] Commonwealth of Pennsylvania Veteran's Compensation Application, dated March 19, 1934

[37] Virginia War History Commission Military Service Record questionnaire, completed by William A. Beverley, November 20, 1919, State Records Collection, The Library of Virginia, Richmond, Virginia

[38] *Winchester Evening Star*, November 8, 1920

[39] *Winchester Evening Star*, November 23, 1918

[40] "Soldiers from Frederick County and Winchester in World War I"

[41] *Winchester Evening Star*, November 1, 1918

[42] *Winchester Evening Star*, January 9, 1919

[43] Eddy, *Winchester and Frederick County in War Time*

[44] Garland Quarles, *Some Worthy Lives* (Winchester: Winchester-Frederick County Historical Society, 1984)

[45] *Winchester Evening Star*, October 4, 1918

[46] www.findagrave.com/memorial/49180497/silas-edward-fauver

[47] *Winchester Evening Star*, December 10, 1918

[48] Unsigned Virginia War History Commission Military Service Record questionnaire completed on his behalf, State Records Collection, The Library of Virginia, Richmond, Virginia

[49] www.findagrave.com

[50] *Winchester Evening Star*, November 15, 1919

[51] Virginia, Death Records, 1912–2014 for John H. F. Golliday; www.ancestrylibrary.com

[52] *Winchester Evening Star*, May 5, 1920

[53] Conversation with Mildred Brumback, July 8, 2016

[54] *Winchester Evening Star*, November 26, 1918

[55] *Winchester Evening Star*, August 21, 1918

[56] Raymond S. Johnson, New York Sate Division of Military and Naval Affairs www.dmna.state.ny.us/historic/reghist/wwi/infantry/369thInf/369InfHistSketch.htm

[57] American Battle Monuments Commission

[58] Grave stone, Wesley Chapel

[59] *Winchester Evening Star*, October 8, 1924

[60] *Winchester Evening Star*, January 4, 1919

[61] *Winchester Evening Star*, March 6, 1921

[62] www.findagrave.com

[63] *The Morgan News*, Friday August 23, 1918

[64] *Winchester Evening Star*, October 15, 1918

[65] *Winchester Evening Star*, November 5, 1918

[66] American Battle Monuments Commission, St. Mihiel Cemetery

[67] *Winchester Evening Star*, October 15, 1918

[68] Interview with Brenda Nelson, July 1916

[69] *Winchester Evening Star*, October 16, 1918

[70] Certificate of Death, Virginia Death Records 1912-2014 for Alex J Nielson, www.ancestrylibrary.com

[71] *Winchester Evening Star*, October 18, 1918

[72] www.Fold3.com/image/322945631

[73] www.fold3.com/image/570027387

[74] Virginia War History Commission Military Service Record questionnaire completed by Charles Hubard Oldham in Salem, Virginia, July 21, 1921, State Records Collection, The Library of Virginia, Richmond, Virginia

[75] *Winchester Evening Star*, August 10, 1922

[76] *Winchester Evening Star*, August 12, 1921

[77] *Winchester Evening Star*, December 30, 1918

[78] *Winchester Evening Star*, July 5, 1919

[79] American Battle Monuments Commission, Meuse-Argonne Cemetery

[80] *Winchester Evening Star*, November 25, 1918

[81] *Winchester Evening Star*, September 6, 1918

[82] American Battle Monuments Commission, Meuse-Argonne Cemetery

[83] *Winchester Evening Star*, September 6, 1923

[84] *Winchester Evening Star*, June 15, 1917

[85] *Winchester Evening Star*, October 5, 1918

[86] *Winchester Evening Star*, November 12, 1920

[87] *Winchester Evening Star*, April 24, 1919

[88] *Winchester Evening Star*, June 8, 1921

[89] *Winchester Evening Star*, October 15, 1918

[90] *Winchester Evening Star*, January 22, 1919

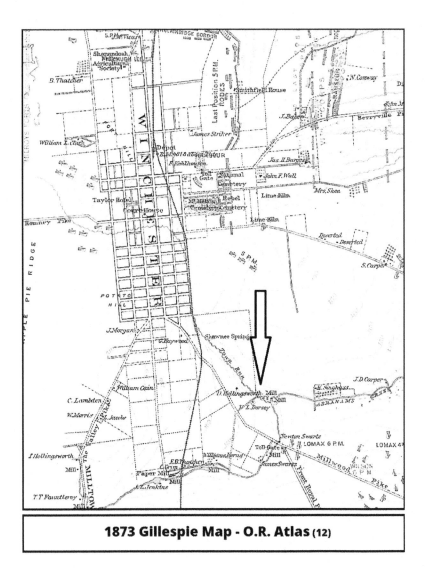

1873 Gillespie Map - O.R. Atlas (12)

Archeological Investigations at Hollingsworth Mill (Abram's Delight)

Marcus D. Lemasters

Introduction

In 2012, members of the Northern Shenandoah Valley Chapter of the Archeological Society of Virginia and the Winchester-Frederick County Historical Society agreed to undertake a preliminary survey of the west and north grounds surrounding the Hollingsworth House and Mill in Winchester, Virginia.

The primary objectives of this field study would be as follows:
- Locate ancillary structures
- Locate residences or quarters associated with slaves reported on the property
- Locate and/or verify the location of the first residence
- Promote visitation and interaction with the public
- Present educational experiences to the Society and public
- Promote and educate the general population in history and archeology

Metal detecting and digging on city of Winchester property, in a very visible area, was a concern for public relations and to possible looting. While on site, every effort was made to show that a legitimate archeological group was conducting the project and to involve the public in education through participation. Local citizens stopped by to see what was happening and ended up devoting several hours of volunteer time. The historical society cleared the project with the City of Winchester, and the city's geographic information system provided the base map used for the project.

Because the property had been abandoned for 30 years in the early 1900s and had seen a lot of public access over the years; the house and grounds were often used for social functions and weddings. Along with its proximity to Pleasant Valley Road, the survey crew expected to find little in the way of diagnostic artifacts and a large amount of modern trash. Experienced detectorists and excavators would be needed for this project. Therefore, any archeological

activities would have to be coordinated around scheduled
activities, be safe for the public, and remain secure.

Site Description

The Hollingsworth Homestead and Mill Complex, also known as
Abram's Delight, is in the city of Winchester, Virginia, at 1340
South Pleasant Valley Road. At an elevation of 691 feet above sea
level, the survey site is bounded to the north by Town Run (the
head waters of Abrams Creek); to the east by the city of
Winchester's recreation area ponds; to the south by parking lots;
and to the west by a four-lane paved road, Pleasant Valley Road.
Currently the following structures are on the grounds: stone house
with extensions, stone mill, mill pond, formal garden, patio, tool
shed, and a gazebo. On the western side of the property there is a
historic log structure that was moved to the property for
preservation and interpretation.

The survey site can be located on the USGS Winchester Quad at
coordinates 17S QD 452 394. Survey components were conducted
in the west and north yard of the Hollingsworth House. Ground
surfaces varied from sparse to thick, short mown grasses
overshadowed by large oaks, evergreens and hedges. For a large
portion of the yard and formal garden, the grounds were evidently
filled and leveled to create a flat area bounded by hedge and steep
slopes to the east, down to the millpond. Some portions of the
original millrace are visible, but were largely destroyed by the
relocation of the town run. The cut of the run creates abrupt and
rocky embankments on the north end of the property. A farm or
access lane is still recognizable, on a north-south axis in the west
yard, lined by large trees.

For its early years, the Hollingsworth complex was outside of
Winchester and some distance into Frederick County.
Advancements in transportation and development soon prompted
annexations by the city to incorporate this area.

Historic Context

In 1728, pioneer and settler Abraham Hollingsworth came to the
Shenandoah Valley with the intent of finding a location to provide
a new home for his family and establish a mill. He found a

location near a series of springs in what became Frederick County, Virginia. Upon receiving a grant for 582 acres, Hollingsworth built a log cabin for his first dwelling, complete with a hand dug well. It is believed that a wooden stockade surrounded the property. Family tradition states that when Abraham first arrived, Shawnee Indians were still in the area and had an on-again, off-again relationship with the Hollingsworth family. The prominent spring became known as Hollingsworth Spring. The first mill was constructed in 1733. Abraham soon began construction of the current stone house, next to the cabin. He died in 1748 before the house was completed and his spouse, Ann, died in 1749. Their son, Isaac inherited the Hollingsworth properties.

Isaac Hollingsworth was a leading member of the local Quaker meeting and planned his house so that it could be used for Quaker meetings. It was referred to as a "mansion" when compared to the log cabins in which his neighbors lived. The builder of the new stone house, Simon Taylor, demonstrated his skills as a stonemason in the house's walls, twenty-two inches thick. One of the interior walls was made with hinges, so the wall could be raised and hooked to the next wall. This made it possible to accommodate large crowds for meetings and was one of the largest buildings in the area. During the French and Indian War, the Quaker Hollingsworth family lived in Waterford, Virginia, to escape involvement in the conflict.

The third generation to occupy Abram's Delight was Jonah Hollingsworth and his family of fourteen. More living space was required. Therefore, around 1800, the west wing, or reception room, was added. He also added a portico on the south entrance, which is no longer standing. Jonah rebuilt the old gristmill and then built a flax seed oil mill, a carding mill, and a shop to build carding machines. In 1778 Mr. Hollingsworth and George Matthews were advertising their fulling and dyeing business that they were starting up on a large scale.

Jonah's son, David Hollingsworth, acquired the properties in 1830 and began a series of improvements. David, a prominent businessman in the community, was known for his love of entertaining. His most spectacular improvement to the grounds was the construction of a large lake on the south side of the house, utilizing the plentiful water supply and increasing the water flow to his nearby mill. A summerhouse was built on an island in the lake and a fleet of boats carried visitors from the shore to the island. In 1833, David married his cousin Eleanor Hollingsworh. More family wealth came to the property in the form of slaves, which had never been used on the property before. The Society of Friends (Quakers) did not allow cousins to marry, so both David and Eleanor left their meeting and joined the Presbyterian church. This is important to the grounds, as it allowed David to make several changes to the house and property. He rebuilt the front of the stone mill and remodeled the interior of the house.

David's three children inherited the properties two years before the American Civil War. The effects of the war greatly reduced the family's wealth, forcing the Hollingsworth family to sell off portions of the property. The size of the property was reduced from the original 582 acres down to the present 32. His daughter Mary is often mentioned in diaries of prominent women in Winchester during the war. Following the deaths of two of the siblings, Jonah Isaac in 1910 and Mary in 1917, Annie retained Abram's Delight. However, she never married and made an agreement to give her two cousins the properties if they would take care of her for the remainder of her life, which they did. After her death the house was unoccupied for about 30 years.

The property was acquired by the city of Winchester in 1943 and has enjoyed a semi- protected status since that time. Winchester purchased the old home and land to preserve one of the oldest homes in the city and to protect the water supply from the spring— also known as Rouss Spring—that they had leased for many years. The Winchester-Frederick County Historical Society spent the next nine years restoring the house and grounds and has occupied it to the present. As the original Hollingsworth properties were acquired by the city of Winchester, the building and development of Pleasant Valley Road, the terrain of the town run was radically moved and modified.

Preliminary research produced no documentation of prior archeological activities, either survey or excavation, for this site. The site had been recorded with the state Department of Historic Resources and Abram's Delight had been part of the society's historic house/structure survey conducted in the late 1980s.

Survey Plan

The site survey plan was developed and implemented in accordance with methodology established by the Archeological Society of Virginia and as presented to students and/or graduates of the Archeological Technician program. Planned archeological activities included mapping of the site, establishing a systematic grid and baselines, surface observation and collection, metal detector survey, shovel test pits, and exploratory test units. This fieldwork was followed up by lab work conducted by chapter members at their lab in Stephens City, Virginia, including: washing, mending, identification and analysis. The report and artifacts would then be given to the Winchester-Frederick County Historical Society's repository.

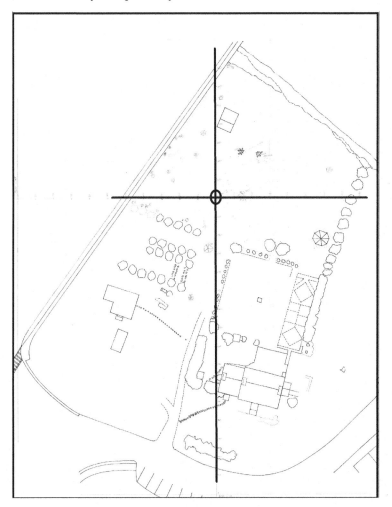

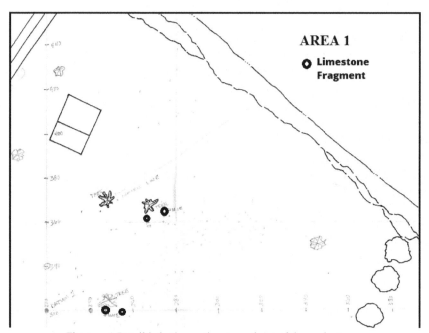

The area 1 Detail is in the northeast quadrant of the project map,
and the area 3 is in the southwest quadrant.

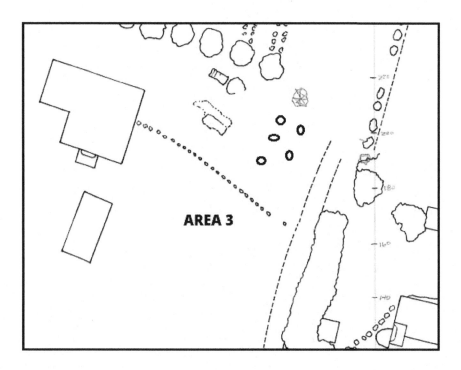

Survey Methodology and Effectiveness

Project Preparation—A geographic information system (GIS) base map was obtained from the city of Winchester's GIS group. This map was set up on a 1 inch = 20-foot scale that was developed from a 2010, 1 pixel = 6-inch orthophoto base. Next, a magnetic north 20-foot interval grid was overlaid on the entire property with the initial grid point of 0,0 to the southwest corner and the east/south baselines outside of the property boundaries. The working south-north baseline was established on the East 220 grid line that bisected the survey area and the working west-east baseline was established on then North 32 grid line on the open rear yard space. These working baselines created a cruciform pattern in the north back yard of the Hollingsworth house that would allow for determining the original landscape slope. At the E220 N320 grid intersection, a stake and enameled plate were embedded to establish the primary datum. Placement of the datum was checked and rechecked with GPS, compass and manual transit and tied to the northwest corner of the Hollingsworth house. The GIS map was updated with notable features from the orthophotography. Small ancillary buildings, trees, shrubs, and hedges were added. Grid line intervals were measured and marked with survey nails along the two working base lines.

To accommodate easier data collection in the southwest yard and Area 3, a second datum was set at 340 degrees, 200 feet from the primary datum; 4 feet to the east of the northeast garden fence corner; in line with the north fence; transit elevation at 62 inches from surface pin to sighting drum.

Artifact Management—Locations of all artifacts recovered in all phases of the study were mapped by traditional transit methods on the English tenths of a foot. The artifacts were cleaned, analyzed, and photographed at the NSVCASV lab at 805 Fairfax Street in Stephens City, Virginia. South's Cataloging System was used for inventory and analysis. A copy of this report and the artifacts were released to the Winchester-Frederick County Historical Society.

Surface Observation and Collection—During this phase, mapping features from the orthophotography were field verified. Any surface features not previously noted were added to the map base.

No easily identified cultural artifacts—nails, ceramics, etc.—were noted or collected. The ground surface of the study area was well maintained and any surface limestone was noted and mapped as anomalies. In relation to other sites investigated in the county of Frederick, loose stones indicated one of two things—spoils from foundation pillars or debris from camp fire pits used during the Civil War.

These stones were found in two specific locations of the site. One area of the north yard had trees with loose limestone at their bases and it is speculated the stones were thrown up against the trees to avoid hitting them with a mower. The second cluster of limestone fragments lay between the Hollingsworth house and the log cabin. These stones appeared embedded in the earth and in a laid configuration of pillars for a structure 10 to 12-foot square.

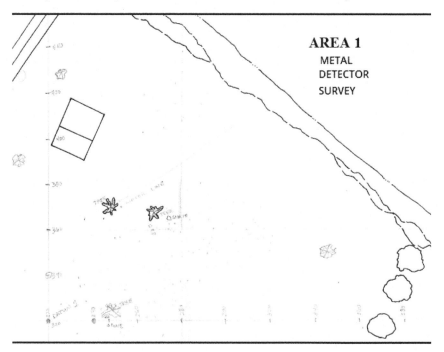

Metal Detector Survey (MDS)—Many of the Chapter's members have years of experience using metal detectors and have worked on survey projects for the Virginia Department of Historic Resources, William & Mary, James Madison University, and various Cultural Resource Management Firms (CRM). Detectorists were instructed to do a random survey and sampling of metal artifacts within the study area. All metal detector locations or hits" were identified with a yellow flag. Non-ferrous objects were flagged but not excavated.

At the detectorist's discretion, if an artifact was deemed to be of diagnostic probabilty it was excavated, flagged in red, and the artifact was bagged with the following information: detectorist initials, item number, description, depth in 10ths of a foot, site ID, and date of detection. This information was included both on the artifact bag and the flag related to it. Artifacts were removed from the site the same day as detection, red flags marked with the appropriate information and the artifact sent to the NSVC lab for processing. All flagged detector locations were photographed and entered into the mapping via traditional transit survey methodology. Isolated metal detector hits and recoveries were found throughout the survey area; however, a large concentration of ferrous targets were mapped in Area 1.

Artifacts recovered during the metal detection phase included the following: Activities Group (23) blacksmithing, gardening, farming, firearms, and storage; Architecture Group (18) hardware, masonry, nails, window; Clothing Group (2) flat buttons; Kitchen Group (12) bottle glass, ceramics, kitchenware, faunal remains; Military Group (5) bullets, uniform parts; Personal Group (9) coins, toys; Stable & Barn (2) harness, wagon.

Shovel Test Pits (STP)—A shovel test pit is a 12 to 14-inch diameter hole that is excavated down to the sterile or sub-soil (containing no artifacts).

To establish the grade or drop in elevation from west to east in the north yard, shovel test pits we excavated along the 320-north grid line or transect at the 20-foot intervals prescribed by the overlying grid. STPs were also excavated from 320 on 20-foot intervals, north along the 220 east transect. A negative STP was a location devoid of any cultural (man-made) artifacts and a positive STP denoted a location resulting in artifact collection. Artifacts were sent to the lab for analysis.

When possible, excavators recorded approximate depth of artifacts. The final depth of the STP was recorded and the information utilized in determining original slope terrain before cultural disturbance.

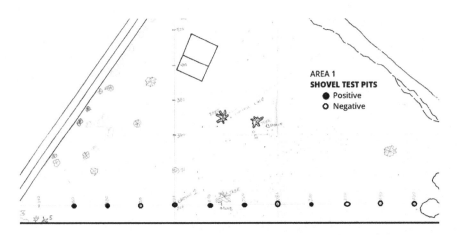

Artifact Results from Shovel Test Pits

STP E140, N320: NEGATIVE; depth 1'2"

STP E160,N320: POSITIVE; Pre-historic (1) lithic flake; kitchen (1) bottle glass; architecture (2) masonry, brick; depth 1'4"

STP E180,N320: POSITIVE; Kitchen (1) ceramic/pearlware; Architecture (1) brick; depth 1'5"

STP E200,N320: POSITIVE; Architecture (4) masonry/plaster; depth 2'2"

STP E220,N320: POSITIVE; Activity (2) redware/flower pot; kitchen (1) pearlware; depth 1'0"

STP E240, N320: POSITIVE; Architecture (1) nail; depth 1'6"

STP E260, N320: POSITIVE; Kitchen (2) ceramic/pearlware; depth 1'4"

STP E280, N320: NEGATIVE; depth 1'8"

STP E300, N320: POSITIVE; Kitchen (3) ceramic/creamware/redware; Architecture (2) nail/cut (1) masonry brick; depth 1'0"

STP E320, N320: NEGATIVE; depth 2'2"

STP E340, N320: NEGATIVE; depth 0'6"

STP E360, N320: UNEXCAVATED

STP E220, N340: NEGATIVE; depth 0'6"

STP E220, N360: NEGATIVE; depth 0'7"

STP E220, N380: POSITIVE; Prehistoric (3) lithic/flakes; depth 0'7"

Test Units—As part of the project, the historical society had requested that the excavations be open to the public and to be interpreted during the Winchester Civil War Weekend. Area 3 where the clusters of embedded limestone were noted during the surface observation phase of the study was selected for this demonstration area. The excavation of exploratory units would be in an area of safe and easy public access. Plus, this excavation would help in identifying the theorized foundation.

An early aerial photograph in the museum shows what appears to be a long shed much larger than the pillar stone configuration. Speculations on the use of the structure ranged from garage, shed, stable, barn, and workshop to a possible location of the original settlement cabin site. In conjunction with the public education effort, the chapter planned two Test Unit excavations to determine dating, use of the structure and foundation type—wall or pillar. Testing with a solid steel probe suggested that a solid laid limestone wall lay just beneath the surface. A title of Feature 1 was assigned to the foundation. The test units would include one suspected corner and a cross section of one wall: TU1 – would bisect middle of east wall; TU2 – suspected southwest "corner" or pillar;

Test Unit 1-Test Unit 1 yielded a total of 294 artifacts: Activity Group (138) gardening, containers, farming, heating; Architecture Group (109) round nails, square cut nails, brick fragments, plaster; Kitchen Group (24) ceramics-redware, creamware, stoneware, glass-bottle, container, animal bone, and oyster shell; Personal Group (2) 1 cent piece, oval eyeglass lens; Prehistoric (13) knapping flakes- chalcedony, gray chert, black chert; Unclassified (7) iron fragments.

The units were laid out so that it would provide a cross section of the foundation and any visible builders trench with the foundation bisecting the unit north and south. As the east half was believed to be outside of the "structure," it was labeled TU1A. And the west half of the unit was given the label of TU1B. The unit was excavated in arbitrary layers with attention to change in stratigraphy and intrusive features. When the Ao (sod) layer was removed, the top and width of a wall was visible and splitting the unit into interior/exterior proved worthy. Often, the artifact content of a structure will differ from outside to inside, and the interior artifact content is more reliable on determining age and use of the structure.

The excavators determined that the stonewall had been dry laid, without mortar, on the period ground surface. No builder's trench was evident. The wall had a width of 16 inches.

The soil and artifacts were mixed throughout the topmost levels of excavation. Even prehistoric flakes of chalcedony and gray chert were mixed into the layers. Not until reaching the base of the foundation, did the excavator begin to distinguish 19th century content from the upper 20th century artifact strata.

In the northwest corner of the unit, a rodent burrow (Rodentia dementia), most probably a groundhog den, cut into the interior of the structure with the opening slating upward to the wall in the east side of the unit. Artifact content from this feature was a mixture of all the layers and time periods.

The sub-soil at the base of the foundation wall had high concentrations of marl and concretions. As is found in other Frederick County prehistoric sites around springs and streams with marl concentrations, prehistoric occupations may be found deeper, mixed in and underneath the marl deposits.

Marl was originally a term loosely applied to a variety of materials, which occur as loose, earthy deposits consisting of an intimate mixture of clay and calcium carbonate, formed under freshwater conditions. Marl is also known as mud marlstone and is an earthy substance consisting of lime-rich mud containing variable amounts of clays and silt that becomes calcified as it solidifies and ages.

Test Unit 2- Test Unit 2 yielded a total of 739 artifacts: Activity Group (109) containers, wagon, harness, hardware; Architecture Group (198) cut nails, round nails, slate, roofing and slate nails, window glass; Faunal Group (87) cat burial; Kitchen Group (316) bottles, bottle glass, lamp glass, faunal remains, ceramics-redware, whiteware, creamware, porcelain, pearlware; Pre-Historic (29) flakes-chalcedony, black chert, grey chert.

This unit provides excavators with a splendid view of a well, dry-laid limestone wall and corner approximately 16 inches wide. As

with the wall in TU1, no builder's trench was evident and the wall was laid on the original ground surface. A higher count of 19th century artifacts in the way of ceramics and cut nails was found within this unit, especially on the interior, (southwest corner). Soils and artifacts were marginally mixed and layering of time marking artifacts could be determined. Minor mixing did not greatly disturb the demarcation between wire and cut nails. 19th Century ceramics including redware, pearlware and porcelain were bountiful.

There were three rodent intrusions in the exterior side of the unit. Burrow or feature TU2F1 contained many pieces of tin cans, broken glass, and building debris. Burrow or Feature TU2F2 was packed full of complete and broken beverage bottles from the early to mid-1900s, evidently a convenient place for disposal of trash. The remaining burrow or Feature TU2F3 was deepest burrow, going below the wall base line was devoid of cultural artifacts, but contained the remains of a domestic cat, curled in a sleeping position.

Additional Research—Research into the written record revealed some historic references to the area that were useful in corroborating events with the archeological findings.

- A local newspaper, the *Winchester Republican* listed the following advertisement in 1861: *"Strayed or stolen from Camp Hollingsworth near Winchester on or about the 10th of September a dark bay horse about 16 ½ hands high, nine or ten years old and slightly hipped – Reward of $10 for delivery at Mr. Jenkin's near Winchester – Capt. John C. Shoup – Winfield Co. B.G. Rifles"* (4)

- The diary of Julia Chase: May 19, 1862 – *She has been ill. Feel much better today, the morning quite cool and a little cloudy, so we propose going to Shawnee Springs. Was at the springs – partook of the cool water, and proceeded as far as Miss Mary Hollingsworth's – went in and rested ourselves* (Note: This was at Rouss Spring – Abram's Delight) and viewed the country, water etc." (4)(6)

- *Mr. Isaac Hollingsworth has erected a splendid brick dwelling near Winchester, contiguous to his fine mills – his yard and curtilages handsomely enclosed with first rate stone walls."* (5)

- The 1850 Products of Industry survey show two water-powered mills in use at the Hollingsworth site with David Hollingsworth being listed as a miller and running a sawmill. (7)

- *"May 15, 1864: Sigel and five of his staff boarded with Mrs. Hollingsworth, and at the end of the week when they were about leaving, Sigel gave her $5 as pay besides taking the flooring of their mill, had camp stools and tables made from the lumber and sold them to their own soldiers. What conduct for a General!"* (4)

Summary and Conclusions

Original Grade and Fill—At the west edge of the study area along Pleasant Valley Road, there is a 3-foot-high embankment between the road and leveled yard and at this point the yard sits at 667 feet above sea level (ASL). The width of the rear yard is approximately 175 feet across. Although the yard appears to be level, it slopes downward toward the east to an elevation of 660 feet ASL, a drop of 7 feet in elevation. At the eastern edge of the yard, the ground surface was built up and evergreens had been planted, date unknown. To the east of these trees the next elevation past a steep embankment measured at 655 feet ASL. These measurements imply that the grade and ground surface were elevated and filled to accommodate a "flat" yard with varied fill depths of approximately 3 to 5 feet. STPs in this eastern area would not reach the original ground surface or grade.

Area One—Distribution. A concentration of 89 uncollected metal detector hits indicates the possibility of either campfire pits from the Civil War or the presence of wooden ancillary structures. Loose, surface limestone chunks could indicate either fire pits of structural foundations/pillars. STPs conducted along the north 320 baseline revealed cut nails and pearlware and creamware ceramics. These artifacts indicate early- to mid-1800s use and occupation. Because no Civil War artifacts were found in the central cluster of metal artifacts, it is speculated that this area served as core domestic use, that could be trash scatter or debris from the slave quarters. Location, distance, and direction from the main house are typical of these types of structures. The 1850 census did list 10 slaves on the property.

Further testing via metal detector recovery and shovel test pits would establish dating and use of the area. Additional artifact collection in this area would also determine if further study by excavating test units are necessary.

Area Two—Civil War Component. The metal detector survey developed a concentration of early Civil War artifacts that are typical to a military camp, i.e. dropped bullets, buttons, and coins. Shoulder scales like the one found were parade and decorative uniform parts that were outdated and quickly disposed of by the soldiers early in the war. A soldier in combat had more than enough to carry and to worry about than drag around extra fancy hardware that needed constant polishing. It was much easier for the common soldier to reply, "oops, I lost it," rather than "I did not have time."

The actual location of Camp Hollingsworth has not been documented or recorded, but it has been implied this early war Confederate camp was in the locale of the springs and Hollingsworth's Mill. The Hollingsworth complex was much appreciated by the local populace during the War and officers from both sides boarded at the Hollingsworth house. The original alignment of the lane to the house can still be seen, as a tree-lined

trace coming in from the north and Winchester. This route would have been utilized by the Hollingsworths going into town and for visitors coming out.

This location would have been ideal for a military camp with good water from a spring-fed stream and off the beaten path. Behind the shed, the edge of the camp begins to show along the old land. The movement of the town run, building of the road system, and the local park probably obliterated most of the remaining camp area. More investigation of this early way camp may

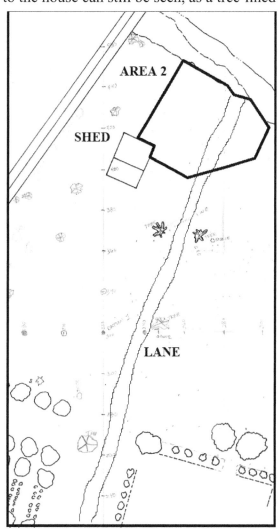

provide interesting information. Exploration of the run, millraces, and the opposing creek bank may yield more artifacts related to this encampment.

Area Three—Foundation Stones. The excavation of two test units in this foundation provided excellent opportunities to interpret archeological methodology, education, and participation to the public. On one day, a local professor from Shenandoah University brought his class to the site for an introduction to field archeology.

The abundance of cut nails implies that the structure above ground was frame-built and set on a solid full stone foundation. The construction of the 16-inch-wide sub walls would have easily supported any sill and frame construction and provided a firm base for floor joists and board flooring.

Trying to determine the use of the structure is very challenging. No fireplace base was found in the two units, but the entire structure was not excavated and a fireplace could be found in other portions of the structure. Artifact content from the bottom or early layers produced several food preparation and consumption items, including a fireplace shove/spatula handle. Throughout the years, the structure saw many other different useS from wagon shed/stable, coal storage, blacksmithing workshop, to gardening/potting shed. The small number of personal items recovered in similar domestic settings was sadly lacking at this site.

Exact dating of the structure foundation was not possible. However, study of the artifacts infers that the main period of occupation and use was between 1820 and 1870. Cut nails and ceramics were instrumental in working up a "battleship" graph, or using a combination of artifact dates and counts to determine a timeframe by small use, major use, and small use. After this period, the use of the structure dwindled away to almost nothing and probably resulted in its abandonment and deterioration. During the 1920s and 1930s animal burrows (groundhog primarily) outside and along the foundation were used by stray animals and filled in by humans with trash and bottles. With the case of many abandoned accessory structures, artifacts in the top layers of soil and on the surface show the structure was used as a repository for junk and trash before being removed and cleaned up during the upgrades to the property in the 1940s and 1950s.

Area Four A and B—Prehistoric Component. One small area near the tool shed in the rear north end of the property yielded some positive test pits with lithic flakes of gray chert. These are secondary flakes created in the knapping or manufacture of stone tools and/or projectile points. No diagnostic artifacts such as points or tools were located during the study; however, the presence of these workshop flakes indicate prehistoric occupation by Native Americans. The area of the springs and streams would have provided these early people with a plethora of food sources and building materials.

During the excavation of the two test units within the historic structure site, prehistoric lithic flakes of chalcedony and black/gray chert were found mixed in all layers of the site. Any future archeological exploration will expand the knowledge gained from these artifacts, their age, use, and possibly their owners. The abundance of this lithic manufacturing shows long and continuous human occupation that reinforces family history handed down from Abraham and Isaac Hollingsworth interaction with the American Indians who were still occupying this portion of the Shenandoah Valley.

Acknowledgments: These members of the Northern Shenandoah Valley Chapter of the Archeological Society of Virginia conducted the physical aspects of the study: Dan Beavers, Robert Frye, Mike Kehoe, Marcus Lemasters, Laura Lofton, David Powers, and Linda Zuckerman. Volunteers on the project were Connor Campbell, Jenny Campbell, Craig Kendrick, David Kendrick, Rachelle Kendrick, Steve Kerry, Jenny Powers, George Schember, and Tim Youmans. In all, the technicians and volunteers contributed 85.6 hours.

References

Clerk of the Circuit Court, Frederick County, Virginia, Deed, 1946.

Davis, George B. *The Official Military Atlas of the Civil War*. New York: Barnes and Noble, 2003.

Diaries, Letters, and Recollections of the War Between the States. Winchester: Winchester-Frederick County Historical Society, 1955.

Kercheval, Samuel. *The History of the Valley of Virginia*. Strasburg, Virginia: Shenandoah Publishing House, 1973.

Kirkland, C. H. *Environs of Abraham Hollingsworth Property*. Certified land survey, 1982.

Lathrop, J. M., and A. W. Dayton. An Atlas of Frederick County, Virginia, From the 1885 Surveys. Strasburg, Virginia: G. P. Hammond, 1997.

Powell, Allen. *Fort Loudoun, Winchester's Defense in the French and Indian War*, Parsons. West Virginia: McCain Printing, 1990.

Quarles, Garland R. *George Washington and Winchester, Virginia, 1748-1758, A Decade of Preparation for Responsibilities to Come*. *Winchester*: Winchester-Frederick County Historical Society, 1974.

———. *Occupied Winchester*, 1861-1865. Winchester: Winchester-Frederick County Historical Society, 1976.

Notes on Abram's Delight. Winchester: Winchester-Frederick County Historical Society.

The Story of Abram's Delight. Winchester: Winchester-Frederick County Historical Society.

U. S. Census. *Schedule of Free Inhabitants*. Frederick County, Virginia, District 16, 1850.

≈

Journal Article Guidelines

The Winchester-Frederick County Historical Society has an active publications program that publishes reprints of local history classics, new books, maps, and an annual *Journal*. The publications committee is always looking for good papers on local and regional history topics for inclusion in the Journal. One of the purposes of the *Journal* is to give local authors a vehicle for their research. All interested authors are encouraged to contact the Society at 1340 South Pleasant Valley Road, Winchester, Virginia 22601, or call 540-662-6550 for more information.

Use the following guidelines in the preparation of your manuscript.

- Provide one electronic copy in Word, and email the draft to the Society at: cshull@winchesterhistory.org
- Use Webster's Third International *Dictionary* for spelling and the *Chicago Manual of Style* (*CMS*) for endnote and bibliographic form. Pay close to attention to the forms for endnotes. The form differs from that for a bibliography.
- Double space all text and endnotes.
- Place endnotes at the conclusion of the article.
- Number all pages.
- Please do not insert photographs into the text; submit them separately on a disc or provide the actual image.
- Provide your name, mailing address, telephone number, and email address (if you have one) on a cover sheet.

The Publication Process

- If you have a proposed article, either give it to a committee member or send it directly to the Society office.
- Members of the Publications committee review all articles for appropriateness and to further the commitment to local history.
- Authors will be notified if the proposed article has been accepted, and the draft will move into the editorial process.

The Editorial Process

- Editing is an important and essential part of the publication process. All articles will be edited for language and consistency of story line. All facts will be checked and where discrepancies exist the author will be asked for clarification. Each author will be provided with the edited version of the proposed article before publication so that any questions raised by the editor can be answered and to ensure that the editor has not altered the author's original intent.
- July 31: submit articles to Society for upcoming year's volume.

About the Authors

William H. Austin is a lifelong student of the American Civil War. He served in the U.S. Air Force as a pilot and public affairs office. Following his service he led various defense technology marketing and communications initiatives, was the marketing director for a University of Texas history center, and was the director of Shenandoah University's History and Tourism Center. Frederick County has been Mr. Austin's home for the past 20-years, where exploring lesser-known Shenandoah Valley Civil War history is a favorite pursuit. Now fully retired, he currently volunteers his services at Cedar Creek and Belle Grove National Historical Park. Among other duties, he conducts primary historical research for the park.

For 23 years **Marcus Lemasters** was Frederick County's GIS manager and IT director. He has been a member of the Northern Shenandoah Valley Chapter (NSVC) of the Archeological Society of Virginia (ASV) since 1989. He obtained his certification as an Archeological Technician in 2003. Archeological metal detector surveys of American Civil War battlefields and colonial sites have always held his interest, however, over the years he has progressively specialized, obtaining vast knowledge, in colonial period sites and analyzing historic ceramics. In 2010, the ASV awarded Marcus the honor of Avocational Archeologist of the Year. Beside archeology, he is a journeyman tracker specializing in the field of human tracking He has completed the Virginia Department of Emergency Management's (VDEM) tracking certification process. Among his many tracking roles and responsibilities, he is a civilian tracking member of the Frederick County, Virginia Sheriff's Office Search and Rescue Team. He is also the secretary of Tracking Resources—Atlantic Coast (TRAC).

Gene Schultz holds a B.A. in history from the College of William and Mary. He serves on the boards of the Handley Regional Library and the Winchester-Frederick County Historical Society. He is retired from the Commonwealth of Virginia. He enjoys collecting 19th century books on the history of Virginia and in assisting researchers working on the history of the Northern Shenandoah Valley.

Index

C

Cadwallader, William Marshall, 50
Campbell, James A., 12
Carr, Lucien III, 50
Carson, Gen. James H., 19
Chapel Hill, 16, 17, 18
Charles H. Willis Post, 36, 87
Clarke, Mr., 24
Clermont Farm ,22
Commercial and Savings Bank, 37
Conrad, Capt. Robert Y., 38, 44, 50, 51, 56
Coolidge.Pres. Calvin, 41, 43
Crook, Gen. George, 11, 12

D

Dettra, L. R., 39
Dix, Isaac Byrd, 51
Dorsey, Capt., 20
Douglas High School, 1

E

Early, Gen. Jubal, 11, 12, 20
Eddy, C. Vernon, 37, 39, 40, 44, 47, 48, 51
Edmonds, Stuart H., 60

F

Fauver, Silas Edward, 51
Fletcher, Thuman, 52
Ford, Benjamin Pierson, 52
Foreman, Lohr, 53
Forsyth, Gen. James, 13

G

George Washington Hotel, 37
Glass, Dr. Robert, 41, 43
Glass, Mrs. Robert, 41
Golliday, John Henry, 53
Graber, Charles Emmett, 54
Grant, Gen. Ulysses, 11, 12, 13, 14
Green, Louisa, 39
Green, Melvin, 39
Grim, George Barrow, 54

M

N

Notes